Last Stanza
Poetry Journal

Issue #7:
Premonition, Coincidence,
Folklore, Magic

Edited by Jenny Kalahar
Amy Brewer-Davenport, artist

Stackfreed
Press

Stephen Roberts' poem "About Those Rickety Vegetable Stands, Seemingly Abandoned" was originally published in *Concho River Review.*

James Green's poem "I Look for a Pizza Menu and Find the Dharma of Buddha Instead" used by permission of Wipf and Stock Publishers, www.wipfandstock.com.

A version of Michelle Blake's "Advent" first appeared in her chapbook *Into the Wide and Startling World,* Finishing Line Press, 2010.

David Allen's "The Day Mom Died" was originally published in his book *(more}*

Mandy Beattie's "The Hill O' Many Stanes" was originally published in *The Purple Hermit,* April 2021

"The Farmhouse" by Lucy J. Madison was originally published in *I.V. Poems* (1st Edition Sapphire Books 2016, 2nd Edition Labrador Publishing 2018)

Premonition, coincidence, folklore, magic.

My scalp tingled when I wrote those words, and as I sent out the call for poems, I couldn't wait to read what would be submitted.

I was not disappointed. Here are poems of voodoo, Native American spirituality, ghosts, witches, fairies, portents, folk medicine, familiars, tree spirits, celestial musings, ancient gods, tricksters, tarot cards, and the unexpected.

This issue begins a new tradition—an editor's choice award for a single outstanding poem. I knew it would be difficult to decide on only one, but I had a much harder time with this decision than I ever could have imagined. I adore every poem!

This issue's award is presented with congratulations to "Caravaggio, Master of Luminism and Shadows" by John D. Groppe.

Thank you, poets, for another amazing collection of stanzas.
Thank you, readers, for supporting these talented writers.

Jenny Kalahar, editor/publisher

This issue is lovingly dedicated to the memory of a former contributor: poet, actor, husband, friend, and father Daniel Godward. He and his words and works will be greatly missed.

The Changeling

Washing out clothes
at midnight in a pueblo
in the south of Spain,
his heart the giant
artichoke left for days

at the bottom of the fridge:
complex, delicate, cold.
He dares anyone to eat it,
yet wolfs hearts whole
as he gulps down food

and never can gain weight.
Years ago, a pack rat Creole
did voodoo in the nursery.
Miss Marie, the cleaning lady,
took his mother's baby boy

home in her shopping bag and
left him as a grigri in exchange.
Doctors and policemen agree:
even the Polaroids don't match.
He wonders if he will ever meet

the child the voodooienne swiped.
This is the only way, they say,
that a changeling ever changes.
The other—that stolid plodder
married to some tootsie roll,

sedated and saddened and fat—
what if he were to touch him
gently on his sleeping back,
his own impish eyes gone soft
with angels conspiring in midair.

Wringing out his wash,
he hangs it across the moon
and shivers inside: in fact,
he hides in the south of Spain
from such a moment as that.

James Nolan

Night Fishers

A shielded kerosene lamp
mounted on an outrigger,
a rag between two sticks
to catch the wind, then off
they go, cutting a glitter
through the inky ripples.

Shy of the sun for years,
I, too, went night-fishing
under my 100-watt desk lamp,
floating medusan and myopic
in my own mercurial liquids,
not a diver but a lure

to symphonies of fins
from windowless depths.
Then I learned to live
by chance of daylight,
to make my way on foot
as I unfurled myself

among the continents
completing the cross
of my migrations,
to arrive at this beach
under a banyan cradling
a nursery of fishing boats

dormant as cocoons by day.
Every evening, fishermen
light their lamps, push off
on the first inspiration.
What they catch tonight
will feed them for a week.

What I caught those years
has fed me for ten,
but dreams wear thin.
Tonight, I slip with them
on paper ships into
the luminous procession.

James Nolan

Ode to My Breasts

Brushing my ribs,
my breasts feel like a ladies'
evening bag stuffed with money,
lipstick and keys, hanging heavy from
its strap, suspended in air, yet
I'm proud to wear these pendulous orbs
like Christmas stockings filled with toys.
There are elegant drop earrings like this, and
diamond necklace pendants.
And somewhere there is a Duncan Yoyo "walking the dog,"
a child hanging in a swing
carving arcs in the air, the pendulum of a clock
marking time, and pink bubblegum stretched
and suspended from a finger.
There is cake batter dripping from the spoon,
rubber bands in repose. And there are reading
glasses and opera glasses suspended from their chains.
And how about a timelapse camera and
calipers to describe their descent over time,
the curve of their swing or the dimensions
of their elongated oval? Of course, it's disconcerting—
they are wet teabags kissing my belly button,
pure white appendages quivering in the air,
wrinkled like crepe, marked like a striped bass,
mammogram pancakes, memories.
Yet I celebrate you,
alabaster orbs, faded jewels,
droopy tulips, steamed cauliflower,
old friends, survivors, mothers of children,
givers of life, badges of honor.
O mammilla! O phoenixes!
O breasts!

Elizabeth Hill
"Ode to My Fat" by Sharon Olds

Elegy for My Mother

This is my elegy not for your polite, public self,
but for the guzzling beast that was you.
You lived ravenously—devouring all to
the very end, elegant in your pure pursuit.
You competed, at tennis, at cards, at love, in everything
with everyone—with your children. You gloried
in the game. Never mind the loser.
Yet you loved fiercely, if all the while scratching the beloved.
This eulogy is left to me, one of the wounded,
because nobody speaks of your ferocious self.
There is silence, and worse, kind words.
It seems I am the only one mourning the appetite that was you.
It falls to me, the one who resisted your pull,
who hobbled, half-maimed, uphill like Sisyphus,
only to tumble back down to your merciless feet.
It falls to me, your loser, your beloved,
to memorialize a woman so bold, so sharp,
so full of purpose, who confused me and
brutalized me only yesterday, on her deathbed,
sweetly, lovingly, kissing me goodbye.

Elizabeth Hill

The Neighborhood

God lives one house north of me.
A recluse, I never see him out.
Not washing his car, mowing his yard, walking his dog,
but his property is immaculate.

Though I've never seen him in person,
He's always been there for me.
I'm a soul in need,
and, right or wrong,
endowed with shameless audacity.

So, when there's something I require,
be it day or night,
ever eschewing propriety,
I go knocking on God's door.
"Excuse me, might I have a loaf of bread?"
Whatever I need mysteriously appears.

Satan lives one door south of me.
Unlike God, he's always out and about.
He roams around his yard with nervous energy,
lawn overgrown with weeds, house a bit distressed.

Odd thing about the devil is that
he always seems to be in need,
and, right or wrong, he's just like me—
endowed with shameless audacity.

Always quick to ask for assistance,
day or night he'll come knocking.
He asks me if I can change stones to bread.
I'll take the rocks from his hands and give him a loaf—
the one I just got from God.
He never thanks me as he scurries away.

Out of the corner of his eye, he peeks over at God's house.
"Is he ever there? No one's ever seen him."
I tell him yes, he's a really nice guy. Always helpful.

I wonder if God knows
I'm the devil's go-between,
and I'm curious if Satan knows
his bread comes from Jehovah Jireh.

Maybe one day I'll host a party.

John Hinton

Some call it a gift

Second sight, esoteric awareness.
The first time when I was five,
pronouncement from a sleeping child:
"Grandma just died."
Hushed and told it was a dream …
until the phone rang.

Eighth grade math class.
My teacher, Miss Bailey.
I felt a shadow.
To a classmate, I said,
"My cousin in the military just died."
Miss Baily said, "Quit talking."
When I got home … two for two.

A bitter cold January day.
Staring out the picture window.
The house was warm, but I was chilled.
Not of body, but of soul.
Something wasn't right.
I thought of Dad.
Moments later, a pale yellow car in the drive.
"There's been an accident …"

A five, a six, an eleven.
I stopped counting because I couldn't
stop sensing, knowing … too much.
I started to feel disconnected,
as if a stranger in this living existence,
an unknown in the deathly realm,
a nomad of the in-between.

A woman at work,
little more than a stranger.
As I walk by her, I feel the pain.
"Don't do it!" the futile thought.
I reach for her hand, she takes mine,
her tears beginning to flow.
"Tell me," as if she had a choice.

9

I cannot explain these things.
The blessing that is curse that is … a gift?
Perhaps you believe my stories.
There's a chance you are scoffing.
But I have something to tell you—
where you're concerned,
I've had a premonition.

I've seen what's coming
for you.

John Hinton

Caravaggio, Master of Luminosity, Prisoner of Darkness
[Editor's choice award winner]

Caravaggio, master of luminism and shadows,
you, with your violent anger and lust for young men
were more a man of darkness than light.
I see you there in your *Martyrdom of St. Matthew*
at the rim of luminosity edging toward darkness,
a man with a dark beard and thick eyebrows
and a shock of hair over your brow
just as the barber whose apprentice you assaulted
testified at your trial and as you painted yourself
often into your work, a collaborator
holding a lamp in *The Taking of Christ,*
as more than a bystander in *St. Ursula's Martyrdom.*
You hoped to hide your incarnadine self
under the purple cloaks of Rome's Cardinals.
For them, you painted a luminous young Bacchus,
a chubby, draped nude young man
with abundant dark hair festooned
with grape leaves and black grapes
and holding a rare glass goblet of garnet wine.
In your *Jupiter, Neptune, Pluto,*
taunting your tormentors,
you flaunted yourself nude as each god,
demanding that we look up at your genitals,
but could not quell your shame and were compelled
to abet the deaths of figures of light.
The pain of your sins must have been great
for you to put your face, mouth still agape
in horror, on the head of dead Goliath,
nature's beast, held aloft by young David,
the type of young man you desired.
A hunted man wanted for a second murder,
fleeing, trading your paintings
for temporary respite, feverish,

forced from your ship, you died
at Porto Ercole and were buried in *oscuro*
and would never know that your troubled art
would shine forth in the world's grand galleries
where viewers bask in the warmth of your luminance,
not noticing the man skulking
at the edge of light and darkness,
of shame and acclaim.

John D. Groppe

The Stockman's Dream

He walks the gentle prairie slope,
green beneath a cloudless sky,
sheep still large with winter fleece,
the lambs bleating, keeping close,
coyotes lean and hungry, held at bay
by two Great Pyrenees standing watch.

He sees the cities burning,
the hordes in flight, the dusty
and brutish soldiers bored by death,
who shoot the dogs and slaughter lambs
until there is nothing left to gorge upon,
the land a waste, the sky gone dark.

He is in deep woods, eluding trackers.
He carries a black-fleeced lamb
through brambles, fording the river,
scaling cliffs, hiding by day, running nights,
Lamb's guardian, last apostle.
Suddenly he stumbles. Lamb disappears.

He ages. Eons flicker by. Lamb returns,
alive through death, flashing
sunlight where the flock is gathering
in a country without borders. They sing
a new song. Lamb leaps, and a river flows
where he treads, the lowlands green again.

The stockman kneels. He is Lamb's darling,
faithful and true—no love desired more.
Their foreheads touch, the holy kiss
like a star exploding to create new worlds,
and finally all sorrows flee
this exaltation of spreading light!

Thomas Alan Orr

Chasing Blue Fire

Gaze into fire. Know it now.
The hottest burn is blue, the heart
of flame, but looking up, we see
the rainbow—wondrous trick of light—
and sense its coolest hue is blue.
Behold the play of heat and light!

"We fished all night without a catch
and came ashore at dawn. We saw
his fire down the beach. His hand
through blue flame beckoned, and we knew.
He called: 'Paidion … children, come
and eat.' The man, the flame, were one."

In summer dusk, a grizzled man
is hunkered over as he plays
guitar. Blue notes like fire leap
from agile fingers, showing how
a thing can be hot and cool
at once, and so we are seduced.

The dark Madonna smiles behind
cerulean veils of fire, sure
of here and now, as angels bend
to hear her sing the rising sun
upon a world that veers toward night.
They bear this music back to God.

The three, the flame, are one. At once
we are seduced, for dawn and dusk
are times when light will tell the truth.
At dark night's edge, where quasars pulse,
we chase the fire feeding life,
the blue flame burning, always bright.

Thomas Alan Orr

Ephemeral

The plant is human. It blooms one night and its fragrance fills the house. The house is a forest in a folk tale. The blossom is intricate and many-petaled. Each petal is a thought, each afterthought a path branching off into darkness. At the end of one offshoot there's a concealed chamber. Sunlight is handcuffed to a bed. The bed is disposable and the handcuffs are made of leaves. Each leaf is a cry for help, a song whose filigree patterns are too complex to follow. Fine green veins mirroring the Milky Way. Dust settles and dawn comes to the rescue. But the flower's already drooping and the floor is stained where the petals have fallen. A foul smell fills the house. So many houses chained to blueprints, slated for demo. Petals collected and pressed between pages crumble in sunlight. Chlorophyll strikes a bargain with preservatives. The display cabinet disappears.

Peter Anderson

Nimbus

In the village of the myopic, it's easy to ignore what you'd rather not look at. Old friends pass each other on the street never guessing what they've missed. Old enemies likewise cross paths none the wiser. The fine print always gets read, but straight lines are constantly losing their edge, softening until someone stumbles. Buildings grow blurry every day at three p.m. When the horizon gets too fat, the sun goes down. Night comes to the village of the myopic and every lightbulb turns into a chandelier, every streetlight a snowflake, every star a smudge, every constellation a cloud. In the village of the myopic, Van Gogh's night sky is no big deal. In the village of the myopic, every backlit lover standing by a window wears a halo.

Peter Anderson

Lois and Rose (I Left Schlichte's Grocery)

I left Schlichte's Corner Grocery with two packs of Topps baseball cards and turned down the alley toward home. Among the duds in the first pack were the playboy who tossed a no-hitter and the slugger who sold Nehru jackets in a Rodeo Drive haberdashery, but the second had Sherman "Roadblock" Jones and the only Vada Pinson I ever collected. This tragedy is mostly about you, Lois, and you, Rose, screaming and fleeing toward a cul-de-sac after looking up from your gossip to find the pimple-faced Were-Brockley shambling toward you. A fistful of gum-dusted baseball cards brandished in the air like a Hammer Studio claw. The fear-summoning toad-like beast croaking with each heavy breath in its ribcage. I had never felt the adrenaline of striking fear in someone else before. Never anticipated the taste of blood. And hackled at being cast as the werewolf in the latest of our hometown's horror stories. The Classics Illustrated version. I took the left-hand fork, fleeing my lycanthropic awakening toward my house across Hill Street to the rough brick on 7th while both of you shrieked at your dead-end folly at the other end of the alley. In the gloaming beneath the chiropractor's wooden privacy fence. I started shaving later that summer. Used my mother's pink Lady Schick without removing the plastic rotary guard. A man-child carrying a full moon within his DNA. I slipped the cards into my back pocket. I began collecting five o'clock shadows that afternoon.

Michael Brockley

Tocayo

You deadhead marigolds as the downy woodpecker lands on the new wind chime and begins pecking on the cap. This summer has settled hot and humid on those who snip flowers with spent-seed coronas. So you reach for a thermos of ice water as the woodpecker continues its assault on the calypso of the wind. With the water just beyond your grasp, you pause and pluck, instead, a scarab beetle from a tithonia leaf. Today you decide to swallow the beautiful jewel, to savor the tincture of its sluggish toxins. Then you capture a black swallowtail flying through a thicket of Queen Anne's lace. Chew upon the dark glory of its blue-black wings. The bird continues its rhapsody, and you notice the insects begin to taste like those words you have tried to read in dreams when you open a dictionary for a language other than your own. *Duende* rises to your mind after swallowing a handful of honeybees. You have ascended to the role of a broken hero who eats garden beauty to reward himself with a new tongue. *Saudade,* longing for a beauty you may never see again from a duskywing butterfly. *Wabi-sabi* from a blue morpho with a torn wing, a palette of anise and brown sugar. Or *shinrin-yoku,* bathing one's flawed soul in a forest. When the woodpecker flies away, you clutch at a bumblebee stumbling through a blanket flower's red-and-yellow stigma to sample your last word. *Tocayo*, Michael, what beautiful people share your name?

Michael Brockley

Trying to Bury My Half-brother
for Roy

First, we dug a grave; regret and guilt our sharp tools, stupidity our long-handled shovel.

Then our father spoke a few words: *He was always asking for it*, he said.

Once we perfected the brown rectangular hole, we laid ourselves beside him. Not our whole selves: each of us slipped out of the skin of the part that had loved him, that had beaten him, that had tried to forget he existed.

We covered them all up. But nothing stays put in the earth.

The little selves climbed out—grey waifs like the shadows of small children. They wandered the rough terrain of the world, searching for us.

They came to our beds and looked down, each of them,
with pity, with ashes.

Our father cried out in the dark and clutched his heart. Had he taken a strap to his son?

But our mother entered the darkness gladly, like a building shutting down for the night. They could never find her there.

As for me, the grey waif lingers. *You were his sister*, she says.

Sometimes she raises her head and sings a hymn about crossing over.
Sometimes she slumps on a stool in the corner and asks again,
as if I should know,
Where shall we all go now for comfort?

Michelle Blake

The Inventors of Absence

First, we followed the animals through the wild scrub
to the upland berries, north to the cool springs,
south to the succulent leaves.

We carried our homes, bound with willow
to our bent backs. Like the turtle,
we were always *here*.

The young began to notice the way
the birds arrived unburdened just as the light
grew longer, how they fed carelessly

and left before the late storms. No calls at dawn,
no long-necked dancers in the shallows.
But where do they go?

Rules appeared: *Everyone*
must carry a house. More and more
shadows slipped past

until, when we gathered by the fires
at dusk, we found ourselves
surrounded by absence.

Michelle Blake

Advent

After all, it was a marvel—
our baby on my belly,
quiet as sky, eyes wide.
Katharine you said,
and spread her hand,
a whole life in that palm.

Six weeks later, she floated
on the shallow pool of sickness
like a husk. We watched her breathing
up and down, away from us.
On the children's ward, the carols
wafted from the waiting room,
ghosts of the holidays—
we kept vigil so our presence
might pin her body there.

Midnight, my turn, the hall,
small stars of light along linoleum,
I start to understand—spirit
made flesh, the miracle,
how we need it for ourselves.

Michelle Blake

The Gourd

after the Taino and Carib origin mythology

From the first gourd came the fish,
brackish water, murky rivers, clouded oceans,
and from a starfish, stars, from a sand dollar,
the moon. Together they made the sun,
who in turn gave birth to the Polishers of Earth,
handlers of seed and cloth, and from the first sedge,
spores enough to plant the spirits.
Soon mountains grew along coastlines
with tints of blue, and from the texture of bone,
whales. Then arrived a conflict of hurricanes,
the peace of turquoise in their eye,
and we learned to read the mood of the sea.

(Many years later—)

We cast a net of silk with our tongues,
but did not know if that would be enough:
I hide a High John in a bouquet of cassia,
you wait until your blood is thickest
before inviting me to bed.

We cannot be sure of the timing.

If I cut a slice of moon just right,
speak the words of the Dogen,
skim my fingers down the small of your back,
and let the flower-scented High John
do its work, connections will form within us.

(Months later—)

She enters our world not with a slap
but a splash of cool river water,
her eyes opening to beadwork and batik.
We will name her in time. Leave us.
We must study the seasons of the gourd.

Michael H. Brownstein

Portent

You watch your last lunar eclipse from the living room chair
by the crystal moon-pendant hanging in the window.
I stand on my deck a thousand miles away, missing you.

It happens in cadence with the song of night;
bullfrogs and field crickets jug-o-rum, chirp-whirr.
There … dee-dee-dee … the rhythmic bursts of katydids

you taught me to hear, then find their green-leaf bodies
hiding in trees. A barred owl calls out, "Who cooks for you?"
Farther up the hill, horses snort and snuffle.

I imagine you naming emerging constellations
as the moon darkens, turns to blood. The Milky Way
brightens, you stretch open your arms, your mouth,

drink in each star, like souls brushing past in the slow
waltz of late summer's breeze. It takes an hour, maybe
two, for you to absorb all the light. Finally gray

shadows creep across the lawn and shiver up your porch steps.

Marilyn Baszczynski

Under the Trees

My fairy-granddaughters, like all wild-animal-children,
hunger for magic. They watch—

legs of adults become tree trunks
when they stand still too long,

the legs grow roots far into the ground
while the girls squirrel-scurry invisible among them.

Sometimes they invite me in, under the old white pine,
to inhale cool aromatic breezes.

Lately, the pine needles are bronzing,
falling in a thick silent carpet. We trace

faint movement under our feet, follow
the tree's essence, deeply down to tentative tendrils

rooting for earth-milk in ancient stores of long-dead
sea creatures trapped by soil, now stone.

Overhead, the trunk is drawn upright by lofty spirals
of hawks and scavenging vultures.

Do fairies sense what the pine is thinking?
Wide-eyed older granddaughter:

It feels so stiff, so tired. Rusty. It can't swing or sway,
like being locked into itself.

Tears fill the younger one's eyes: *It's thirsty. And dying.*
Later, I come back out alone. I hold a glass of water to your lips.

Marilyn Baszczynski

Lantern

Old women warn of following the will-o'-the-wisp
on black nights over moors,
to stay on the path,
to not go deeper into the woods
where limbs creak overhead.
But there is a certain peace in the quiet darkness
once you've left the path.
The women mutter because they are afraid,
afraid of those who would seek a new path
because it's so different from their own.

I walk in the woods and over moors.
There is nothing to fear in the dark but
 the mutterings of crones.
Lantern lights are possibilities,
a welcome,
company on a journey you didn't know
you needed to take.
Stare a little longer,
a little harder into the deep dark,
and I will guide you by lantern
further into these woods.

Say Davenport

Flowing Like a River

At every step,
I suffer
yet keep going
in my own way

Like a river,
life flows neck-deep
with a heart full of sorrows
towards the sea of ending

Only death is the receiver
of all complaints,
so life heads for death

Guna Moran

Research that Matters #19

"Frequent travel makes people happier by 7 percent."
from "Findings," *Harper's*, March 2021

If you trim your toenails
once a month,
you will live, on average, 1.2 years longer
than those who trim toenails every six months.

Eating breakfast in bed,
even sporadically, makes a couple
feel eleven percent closer.

Having your own vegetable garden,
regardless of the type of vegetables planted,
will cause your hair to turn gray
at a slower pace than normal.

Being kissed at least three times daily
allows you to remember your good dreams at night
at a rate 6.7 percent greater than
those left unkissed.

And for some unknown reason,
people who remember their good dreams
are better drivers, smile more often,
leave larger tips, and touch the faces
of their loved ones whenever they can
or whenever it's appropriate.

David James

Rapunzel

It all began with desire for lettuce—
even the stolen variety
would do for her—
strange, uncontrollable pregnancy cravings—
                driving her to the raggedy edge
of the precipice of no certain return. Did she

ever suspect the witch would hoodwink her—
snatch away from her the rosy child
like an innocent cabbage (even
before it had been weaned from its mother's

heavy, milk-laden
breasts)? After all,

what use could the witch have had for a
golden-haired girl languidly watching suns
rise and wax and set day after day in that insular,
inaccessible tower?

Rapunzel
could have redeemed herself (if
she had only known it) with her own hands,
her own hair—by extension, her own brain
(such a blonde bimbo,
you'd think). After all, the prince was
completely useless, and what's more, extraneous (in
this narrative context), for he was no
redeemer—indeed, merely
the void that mirrored Rapunzel's [v]acuity;
          [excision of the virgin from the phallic tower
              being the vulgar form of redemption].

"Hey, nonny, nonny …" she would sing
all day, braiding and unbraiding locks of golden hair (but never
upbraiding the witch or the prince, who were the same to her,
just that the latter could scale the tower
              with greater, longer-legged, penised alacrity)—

"Hey, nonny, nonny, where is my Johnny?
Oh, Johnny-come-lately …."
She was a caged bird, singing
for her cold supper, waiting apathetically
for the witch to come home: "Rapunzel,
Rapunzel, let down your golden hair!"
when she had the option to refuse, knowing
            the witch had no broomstick with which to beat her into
bruised compliance.

Hiromi Yoshida

The Ride

A forty-minute drive on four tires
in a dinged up gray Silverado,
220,000 accumulated miles
powered by gasoline combustion.
Hauling ass
and two bicycles to a forty-minute ride on two tires,
sturdy frames with thick-rubbered traction
powered by human steam,
but raindrops on the windshield
tapped out an ominous message in bike code:
"Go Home"

We disregarded the warning,
hoping for an intercept of parched atmosphere
to drink up the rain,
or a delay, at least,
pretending that God would notice
and grant a dry, healing ride.
A seven-mile loop through the woods
with its ups and downs,
curves and organic hurdles,
birds and deer and snakes
mending our bodies
engaging our senses
and calming our hearts.

We rolled the bikes off the tailgate
and pinched the tires for give.
                check
Squeezed the brakes lever's for catch.
                check
It's all good.
Big thumbs-up in front of a pretend sunny greenscreen
that eclipsed a blackening sky.

We imagined an enthusiastic wave of a green flag
and accepted a circulating myth that trees and leaves
would perform like roof shingles with a twenty-five-year warranty.

The buckets tipped five minutes from the gate
as we passed the sign that screamed judgment
above the racket of the downpour.
"Do not ride on wet trails."

The one-way path transformed into a raging river.
The torrents drenched our t-shirts and shoes and underwear,
but we kept riding to find the end,
disregarding the giant puffballs and the lush forest view
while paying fanatical attention
to the sensation of mud
spattering on our backs
and shins,
the wind chill,
and the saturation of our socks.

We found a shortcut,
a faint crossover to the loop-back in the drenched weeds,
cutting our ride in half.
We pedaled the slippery trail,
our wet tires squealing past our pinched brake pads.
We emerged from the submerged trail into the parking lot,
back to the gas engine in twenty soggy minutes,
and agreed—
it was a good ride.

                                        Theresa Timmons

Chopin's Rooms

When I hear Chopin's *Waltz in B Minor,*
I imagine going from room to room.

In the living room, I sink into the sofa, the sustaining pedal.
The TV keeps the tempo.

The bathroom toilets are bass clefs.
The piano showers cascading notes.

On the dining room table, our laptops sit open.
We face each other without speaking,
a silent rest.

On the bench, I keep my pills that make me feel sharp or flat.

Our porch is an octave higher than the street.
A rising and falling of stairs.

In the kitchen, I cook lasagna. You open a bottle of Merlot.
Dinner is the crescendo of our day.

The bedroom is the refrain we keep coming back to,
where we sleep and dream of Paris and Chopin.

Marjorie Sadin

Cassie

they said she knew
the day you'd die
and would invite you
to share the tattered seat
of a rustbucket in the alley
behind her daft mother's shed
and demand a dollar
not to tell you
cackling through black teeth
cold talons gripping your arm
barely past 20 yet elders
steered clear of that hovel
and when we pressed them
whispered of the time
an anxious bride
brought her GI's photo
and watched the bony hand
scrawl a date across it
the widow they said never again
knew sleep free from dreams
of green eyes behind lank hair
seeing things
seeing what tempted as it terrified
seeing that for which
we cherish blindness

Dan Carpenter

Emily Nobody

No, she would not profess
to faith at Mount Holyoke
Female Seminary. Yes,

she would be true to
herself, to a life
deepening within. No,

she would not marry,
would she, except to
the art she carved

with pen onto scraps?
She would stay home
and travel to Tunisia.

She would keep quiet
and ride the volcanoes
erupting daily in the house

of the Self. She would
write herself into
the most singular

Nobody of all. Some-
times there was more
ferocious drama going

on in Emily than
in the entire nation
as she stayed home

to mind the business
of interior circumference.
Who among her tiny

circles knew what
was going on in
Emily unless they

received a quaint note
with a compressed
word horde explosive

coiled inside? Who
but those who after
she left us read

the fascicles she
stitched together
with a stiletto pen

felt the force of her
devotion to the life
of the soul that

raged within as she
witnessed her own
private Civil War?

                              Norbert Krapf

Your Muse

I hope you have or find your muse, someone or some place to take
you to your deepest self and discover your greatest gift, whatever it
may be. I hope you have or meet a Robert or a Bobbie or a
Zimmie or a Dylan who moves you beyond yourself and brings
you into your powers. May you have an Echo or a Suze or a Joan
or a Sara or an Isis or a Nettie Moore or a Girl of the North
Country who draws you out of the darkness in you and transforms
it into the light of vision and bestows meaning on your life.
Someone who gives you shelter from the storm, someone who
touches you with love, someone you want and who wants you, a
sad-eyed lady of the lowland who listens to what you have to say
and turns your sadness and sorrow into awareness and
understanding and the gift to speak for others. May you find
someone who releases you from your sentence and lets you see
your light come shining from the West down to the East. Someone
who keeps you forever young by kissing you on the lips and plays
a song that lifts you outside time and takes you dancing with one
hand waving free. May you find and follow your tambourine man
who sings you into the mystical moist night air where you look up,
from time to time, in perfect silence at the stars and feel on your
skin and see with open eyes the light of the stars shining down on you
blessing who you are, all you know, all you shall become.

Norbert Krapf

Five Found Remedies of my Maternal Ancestor, August Betz

1. Effective Secret Medicine for all Illnesses

If you boil a piece of pork meat
in a sick person's urine until it's gone

and then boil it in more of his
urine and then again a third time,

then feed that meat to a dog or pig
or some other animal. The sick patient

will get well and the animal will get
sick and die. Do not feed the meat

to the animal of someone you
care for. Feed it to your own dog

or one you can tell is as shiftless
and worthless as a smelly skunk.

2. On Banishing Hernias

Take orchis satyricon, orchis testiculus,
or orchis morio, whichever you can get,

and dig the plant out of the ground
with leaves, stems, and roots three

days before the new moon, but always
toward evening or night. Tie this plant

to the hernia so it gets warm, then put it
in a place where it does not dry up.

Do this again on the second and third
evening. Thereafter, before the moon

begins to wax, put the plant in the ground
in a spot where's it's sure to grow.

As it grows, the hernia will disappear.

3. To Stop Wetting the Bed

If a person can't stop pissing in bed,
he should take a young blind mouse

and burn it to a crisp in the fire,
then mash it into a powder,

mix it into some kind of food
and eat it. Works every time!

4. For Colic

Take 1 ounce "Devil's dung" [asafoetida]
dissolved in boiling water and 4 quarts

manure and about 1 pint linseed oil. In case
the colic has not stopped in 4 hours, one

has to repeat the above every 4 hours.
If the horse has eaten strong fodder,

blood has to be let from the artery
in the lung. It's tried and proven!

5. For Consumption

It is good to eat a head louse
on a butterbread sandwich

3 Fridays in a row.
This really does help!

Norbert Krapf

Betz family reunion (1913) on the John L. Betz farm

About Those Rickety Vegetable Stands, Seemingly Abandoned

When the radishes were pulled, early May,
someone down the dirt road screamed.
No missing-person report was filed,
though a local who didn't matter disappeared.
Rumor has it there are connections in the soil,
tangles of hysterical tentacles reaching.

In the proper week, the proper time, we hunt
wild asparagus with handguns, hollow points,
and old rusted butcher knives off the back porch.
It's best to be prepared when the chips are down,
your number's up, or the weather's about to change.
We don't trust asparagus as far as we can spit.

And spit we do when the tomatoes turn.
Best to shine them up a bit before hauling them
off like severed heads to our fruit and veggie stand.
It's how we make ends meet when there are no ends.
Summer heat, humidity, dust, and horrible thoughts
go hand in hand when the love-fruits turn blood red.

                        Stephen R. Roberts

What the Night Tells the Day

Where is your fortunate light,
the easy answers in bold outline,
the warmth of certainty,
the compliant sun?

Darkness gives birth to all philosophy.
Secrets rest in black hollows
like hissing beetles with phosphorescent eyes.
The night disturbs,
the night brings doubt,
the night questions,
the wind whispers challenges
on night-bird wings
and awakens a horde of dark creatures
that live only in the night,
their scrabbling, scratching feet
vibrations felt on the tongue
and the nervous tendrils of the spine.

Why is the day so satisfied
with its brief moment
in the eternity of the night?

Patrick Kalahar

Underneath

Fallen leaves paint the ground.
Once living green things of air and sky,
now multi-hued corpses in sad panoply.
I drop to one knee for a closer look
and realize that this gesture
might be construed as an act
of reverence or supplication
for the silent dead.
But the leaves are not silent.
There are rustlings and vibrations
and murmurs that might almost be words
in some unknown language.
I am surprised with a tremor along my spine
that might be fear or something else.
I brush away the leaves with my hands
and discover—like a modern Columbus—
another inhabited world
as hectic and divergent as my own.

Ants and grubs and beetles and worms
and millipedes surprised by the light
and scampering for the damp and dark—
a teeming city of its own.
And now a larger disturbance.
The leaves are moving by themselves.
A field mouse pops his head above the leaves,
nose and whiskers twitching many questions,
eyeing me and the freshly uncovered food.
I quickly brush back the leaves
and repair the disturbance I have brought.
I'm happy in my discovery,
but I don't want to be a new Columbus:
destroyer of worlds other than my own.

Patrick Kalahar

Rhubarb Monarch

Transplanted from my childhood home
to a new suburban ranch house,
she barely grew.
Small mound of green
came up each spring.

When my parents downsized to a condo,
she was moved to our family cabin on a lake,
foreign soil where she refused to thrive.
When the place was sold,
Dad divided her roots into thirds,
sent each of us home
with a paper-wrapped crown.

Season after season
my inheritance increases,
cerebral mass erupts early,
yields luscious ruby stems,
leaves the size of soldiers' shields.
All summer she rules her corner,
sends up flower stalks
tall as a sovereign's staff.

I think the queen prefers
to be left alone,
likes lots of space.
Too much attention,
she abdicates the throne.

Jan Chronister

My Magic is a Norwegian Forest Cat

My magic is a Norwegian forest cat
weaving the endless saga
of blue-cream and tortoiseshell ferocities

O what unquiet and whispery fur

My silver witchcraft finds
its bluish rune path
in and out of the trees

O the fury of large wild cats

In the imaginary Pacific
coral tree forest,
their bones are heavy and Saturnian

The thick Loki tail of my green frog
Sorceries is long and bushy.
My silkiness shines like a milky quartz

A hunter at heart,
I leap into your head
to plant your angel aura dreams

By my enchanted ancient oak,
ringed by strange old standing stones,
my purring awakens a sleeping dryad

I die a little during shedding season

Diana Thoresen

Tether Me

for Jenny Sawanohk Sutherland

Her roadside creek is a trigram of
vanishing duck feet.
Perhaps she is gazing at a soy ritual candle and an oracle deck.
Her weavings find their way

Into sweetgrass words and roaring rivers

Untethered snowflakes.
A vulnerable rare eagle sits on the mud in Atlantic Canada,
same as my untethered albino heart

It is a recycled butterfly

I remember the dreamer, and how every tree is an altar to her.
My wounded whiteness, my rabbit fur bristling with emerald rain:
it all has vanished into ruby reds, yellows, and purples.
The nights are getting longer

The Feather Keeper sings to blue beads and fall leaves

                              Diana Thoresen

Counseling

Everyone tells me their darkest secrets.
They don't mean to, but they do.
They always have, they probably always will,
but who am I to listen? To comment?
My nails dig into the mahogany façade
of the chair in which my body has been propped
while a woman tells me she wants to die.
Me too, my mind betrays all too readily,
but my face has been etched by years and layers
of porcelain and papier-mâché.
My eyes have long since turned to currants of
self-loathing and contempt.

The straw lining my stomach
pokes through holes in my pressed shirt,
but these people do not say anything,
maybe out of respect
or that innate desire to
avoid embarrassment at any cost,
for I am authority.
I am authority?
The thought amuses me as I
remember what a heartbeat sounded like
in my now deaf ears.

Time has passed without my awareness,
and now a husband sits in silence
as his wife paces around the table
in the center of my tomb.
His voice screams in my head:
Please tell me I am okay,
I just want to be okay,
but I do not speak to him.

Instead, I relish her contempt
and enjoy the murder,
as it is not happening to me—
not this time.

The last person shuts my door and
turns off the light,
and here I rest,
my mind no less active
than when I was not alone,
but also, no more.
The void is comforting.
I can float.

Outside, the world ends,
and it bears no meaning
to my existence in this dark room.
My empty head falls to the floor.
I am not written into a book
for posterity.
There is no posterity,
no future.
Just me
in this room
in pieces,
but ready to listen
to the now extinct.

Matthew Whybrew

The Day Mom Died

The day Mom died, my doorbell rang
twice, two times in the afternoon.

But when I bounded from my chair,
there was no one there
or anywhere near
as I scanned the scene
for signs of a prank or the post.

After the second signal,
I tested the bell for a short
or some other cause.
But it worked just fine.
No gust or glitch had set it abuzz.

Hours later, I got word
Mom departed this cold world.

My wife suggested
Mom stopped by our island,
which swarms with ghosts,
to say goodbye to her oldest son,
one child absent from the last bedside.
And I just shrugged,
and would still, except—

The day they turned our mom to ash, the doorbell rang again.
And her grandson answered only to find no one waiting to come in.

In the months that followed, the doorbell never repeated its
eerie ring, sounding only to announce a package delivered
or a neighbor stopping to say "Hi."

I guess Mom said her final goodbye.

David Allen

Sad Ride

The tired cabbie was about to end his shift.
It was nearly midnight, storm clouds
hid the moon and there was a chill in the air.
As he turned a corner in a run-down part of town,
he saw a woman holding a baby and waving at him.
He stopped and she slowly slid into the back seat.
She sobbed as she asked him to drive
to a nicer, newer, neighborhood.
Once there, she asked the cabbie to wait
while she got money from her husband.

Ten minutes passed and the cabbie
walked to the front door and knocked.
A sleepy man in black pajamas answered.
"I'm sorry, sir, but your wife said she was
getting money to pay for the ride."

The man nodded and gestured for the driver to wait.
When he returned, he paid the fare
and gave the cabbie a large tip.
"I'm sorry," he said, shaking his head.
"My wife and daughter died in a fire years ago.
I've moved several times, but she still finds me."

David Allen

I Look for a Pizza Menu
and Find the Dharma of Buddha Instead

Heading south on I-75
somewhere between Calhoun and Kennesaw,
I pull into a cheap motel for the night,
the sort of place you'd find
a wide selection of porn for rent on the TV
and a Gideon's Bible on the nightstand.

After a hot shower, I look for a pizza delivery menu.
None in sight, I try the drawer to the nightstand.
No menu. No Gideon's. Instead
is a book called *The Dharma of Buddha.*

I am ignorant about many things,
a condition I now accept as chronic,
but I have heard about *karma,*
so I begin reading the pages on the left side,
the ones in English. On the right are rows
of symbols sketched in precise, delicate strokes.
Not Chinese—I heard they write vertically,
the way some poets do.
I accept on faith
the left side means the same as the right
and start dog-earing pages—
a chapter on *Causation,*
another for *The Middle Way,*
which sounds a lot like Aristotle.
A coincidence, maybe.
Or maybe the Hand of Providence.
I cannot know these things.
For future reference, I flag chapters on
The Search for Truth
and *Impermanence and Egolessness.*

Vanity of vanities, all things are vanity ...
all rivers go to the sea, sayeth Qoheleth.
How far did the prophets, the ones of the Levant,
travel in their caravans? To what lands
did the stars they followed lead them?
What did they learn?
The magi who came from far away in the east,
how far to the east was their origin?

The index intrigues me most.
Page number and line for
five things no one can accomplish in this world, and
where to find *four states of unlimited mind.*
Under the heading *Mental Training* is a fable:

how one will find teachings for human life
wherever one goes.

                              James Green

Note: Text in italics are quotations from *The Teaching of Buddha* (Bukkyo Dendo Kyokai, Tokyo, Japan, 1987), except for the one from the *Book of Ecclesiastes* that is excerpted from the *New American Bible*, Oxford University Press, 1990).

Autumn Accounts

They say it's never too late, what with
the late President's skydive for his 90th
and the hundred-year-old water-skier
who bobbed and waved from my fridge
till his photo yellowed and frayed.

But it is probably too late to train
as an astronaut or concert pianist, too late
to freeclimb Half Dome or take up
oral surgery. And it's surely too late
to die young.

Still, there may be time
to enter the longing and give ourselves
to what we become
when we turn in its light:

Pitcher of twilight,
angel of glass,
a grasshopper the size
of a young boy's heart.

A labyrinth of stones, like the one
we discovered in the hills—
that slow-walk to nowhere,

the very same nowhere
we were getting to
so fast.

Prartho Sereno

Memegram

A variation on a meme,
sent out from the planet, shakes
at the international sand art.

The Earth quake erases
to begin again with truth,
perhaps one that bridges enough
to lived experience for a century or so.

Grounded oversized brains
assert, explore, disavow on two feet.

The gravity throughout the process holds
onto great expectations for a species
scratching granite while lost in space.

Though the upside down etch-a-sketch
mirrors beach and desert
and attracts gray areas under a sun,
transparent plastic breaks down after a cry.

Rich Murphy

Biochem Lab

After the volcanoes choked on virgins
to appease the gods, and firstborn
did the trick keeping the death numbers
down for a while for cultures, old goats
stuck out necks for whole communities.

Then finally, the world shrank
for the people who brought the bucket.
And as though the sailors and families
believed that the color-sacrifice
sufficed as innocent enough

entire races morphed into rotten eggs
and were thrown under buses
a dozen at a time, all day, every day.

From bone broth and muscle greed,
the primordial soup fed carrot and sticks
and seasoned with resentment, winter, envy.
The jellyfish able to take shapes
set foot on shore and never looked back
for empathy, cooperation, imagination.

Rich Murphy

Pilgrimage
for Pat Fargnoli

Of course the stone, warmed by the August sun,
was just the spot a cat would select to loll
and purr and entice the woman to pat him.

But it was a flat gray gravestone set flush in the ground,
and it was a black cat, and it lay sprawled on the stone
and it stared off into the gray distance toward the hills.

And it was Robert Frost's gravestone, in Vermont,
and the woman was a poet from New Hampshire.

And of course the cat never left that stone
all throughout the woman's silent afternoon vigil.

And perhaps at some point she laid a flower on the stone,
and perhaps as she left, the cat wove between her feet.
And perhaps by the time she reached her car, the cat
had vanished.
        And then did a dark gray cloud
obscure the sun? No, of course not;
that would be too much, don't you think?

Roderick Bates

The Maple

Last night before sleep,
I remembered our week
at the rented cabin
in the Laurentians.
I thought most
of how you looked that first night
when you stood in the middle
of the bedroom floor
and unbuttoned your dress,

how with one quick shrug
it slid quietly to the floor
and pooled scarlet at your feet.

Had I known
it was all you were wearing,
I might have been bolder at dinner,
or as we sat beside the parlor stove.

In the yellow light
of the kerosene lantern
on the bedside table,
you looked like Venus rising from the sea,
though there was no coyness
in your uplifted hands—
not then, nor later that night.

This morning when I wake,
I look out, as I do these days,
to the old maple in whose shade
you used to read and fall softly asleep.

I see you in the Fall display—
that lone tree, branches raised,
with a circle of red beneath
where it has dropped its leaves
and stands before me
in its simple beauty
which needs no adornment.

                                        Roderick Bates

Ruthie

At four-and-a-half, she would tell fantastic stories,
claiming she was reading her brothers' dreams at night,
insisting her weird and hilarious tales were theirs,
taking no credit for the visions she described.

She was silent so much of the day
that we came to know her primarily through her breakfast tales.
We watched her fork as it separated eggs and potatoes
to help her illustrate which way the red mice ran.
A tiny finger in her milk was an elephant
drinking from a purple pond,
her flowery paper napkin fluttering to the floor
was a kite-winged golden bird at dawn,
and jellied toast became a magic carpet
floating on the evening's silver clouds

At age five, she began to read and write.
She would never tire of her lessons with fat pencil or crayon stub.
It tickled her that a baby "j" had a dot but the daddy "J" did not,
and that the letter "y," if you didn't look at it
was exactly like a question.

By the age of six, she was swept up in writing,
but that writing began to silence her again.
Her constant companions, her notebooks, heard endlessly from her,
but the breakfast table was dull.
And even though her eyes still darted
between her buttered French toast and the syrup bottle,
every story was saved for those intimate blank pages, instead.

Her brothers would sometimes ask,
"What did I dream last night, Ruthie? Where did I go?"
Her only answer was a secret smile.
She wouldn't tell.

She refused to say
even as her littlest brother turned red-faced
and nearly cried at the loss,
not wanting his breakfast after such a cruel denial

By age ten, she was beautiful but pale and thin and delicate.
Her fork stopped moving.
She didn't eat.
Her hands stayed balled tight.
Her feet began to give way too many times and
her eyes forgot to close or forgot to open.
You couldn't tell anymore if she was creating—
her sweet face remained a blank.

Desperate, I dug through her drawers,
under her dolls and in her closet.
I gathered her writings by the armful,
and as I tried to feed her breakfast in bed—
soft yellow eggs that she mostly refused—
I made her listen to her own stories,
trying and trying to remind her of who she really was.
Starting with the messiest scribbled sentences I could find
and reading forward in time as her penmanship matured on the pages,
I told her about her very own rhinoceros, fat and blue
under his rhinestone saddle.
About those trips on asteroids they took to the planet Corn Flake,
where the spider kings ruled atop their cereal box thrones.
I read about her best friend, a motorcycle-riding fairy named Herman,
who would grant wishes only on Sundays, at ten in the morning,
if it was raining, and only if those wishes were for very nice things.

On and on I read, willing her listen,
watching her eyes for recognition, for a spark of impish light.
I fed all of it to her even when she took too little food,
until I got to a story about a little blonde girl named Ruth
who had sought out a terrible witch in the haunted woods—

a witch who had given her a potion to make eating impossible,
a potion to make her atone
for the loss of her mother's favorite necklace
that Ruth had dropped, quite on purpose,
into some forgotten puddle of mud.

And so, finally understanding,
from that day on I fed her the antidote of forgiveness,
sprinkled understanding like sugar on her pancakes,
mixed mercy into orange juice as I read to her
about a retired Florida swamp monster named Harry,
about an antique hat that changed form as it passed from head to head,
and about an undersea dragon who was lonely for the dryness of fire.

I then ended each tale with my own, true story of forgiveness
until she believed me and her eyes finally looked steadily into mine.
Until her mouth chewed faster,
until she held the fork herself
to eat and to divide the eggs and potatoes as I read,
until her legs grew strong enough for her to run away from me
back into the real, green-grass world,
and then fast, fast back into my open arms again,
her bright eyes smiling up at me with that familiar secret smile.
And as we walked where the woods were never haunted,
she told me fantastic, believable stories
all about my dreams.

Jenny Kalahar

The Ghost in the Wound

The glorious pine is cut,
shaken,
tied,
hauled and heaped with others onto the back of a trailer,
their fragrance smothering and beautiful.
A gentle friend from a faraway country
has come to witness the barbaric ways we celebrate,
to see central-heated homes trimmed inside and out
with excessive red, white, green light,
to be offered more than she would ever want to eat,
and to listen to generic piped-in carols
while crushed by crowds of mall shoppers.

Tonight, she blinks dark, troubled eyes.
Crackling bonfire flames behind her
are like unfurling wings of orange flame
she brought with her in case of a chance for flight,
and I wonder what she thinks,
how this meshes with the messages
the missionaries repeated.

Fresh trees slung onto the back of a hay wagon
seem to hurt the most.
She stood near one,
petting its trunk with borrowed mittens,
fighting against sorrow.
I called for her that we were going,
but I think she saw what I did then:
a spiral of grayish-white
hushing from the razored end of the pine:
a ghost reluctantly emigrating
by way of wound.

Jenny Kalahar

Magical Lullaby

Larkspur. Wolfbane. Lady's slippers,
lush and fragrant; hush, now,
little one wrapped in wolf's skin.
Fox fur. Adder. Anaconda. Asp.
Paperwhites forced in winter,
Night sky of sighs. Lies. Murmurs.
Murmurations of starlings, skein
of goslings, glint of goldfish.
From the heights, satellites
fail, flail, fall.
Feral Mars rises over floods,
lichen litmus, blood, sweat, semen;
Romulus and Remus at the wolf's tit.
Latin, Lapp, Lettish, Limbu. Language
found. Language lost. Say: Silkworm.
Spikeworm. Dust. Worms. Say
moonbeam, hornbeam, high beam,
hope. Feckless. Ferrous. Fools' gold.
Shooting star. Stalk.
Snowdrop. Maize and millet.
Crocus courage in its season.
Hush now, little one—do not weep.
Let me sing you my song,
little tree frog to be;
listen and let my words
glisten you to sleep.

Michael Ansara

Now and Then

I lie under a scurrying sky,
gazing, thinking about chance,
destiny, danger, and the gathering
clouds of 1914 and 1913 and 1912—
did horses, grazing in green pastures,
shiver, sensing the coming shudder
of earth, split of sky, the replacing
arrival of tread and tank?
Did the grass quiver, anticipating
bloom of shell, churn of mud, slash of trench?
Did those dancing under stars or standing
together in the velvet dark feel
the wind accelerating, did the scaffolding
of their bones suddenly wrench,
chill and shake—
        or, like me today
and yesterday and tomorrow,
did they too rise to the morning, glower
at the uneasy news, cling a moment
longer, lingering in the embrace of the beloved,
silently frightened, faintly, oh so faintly aware
of all that can be summoned
by a single shot
        or a madman's call.

Michael Ansara

Under the Lunar Eclipse

Heaven hemorrhages
Life leaks lunar lament

I am bloodshot in my third eye
My tears soothe the irritation

Stroke of the witching hour
Spectator of shifting satellites

Only a trace of light
Forms a slight crescent

Only a sleight of hand
Forms the traits of chaos

I offer gifts to ancestors
This season of the witch

We of the ways of wizards
Make sense of the chaos

Working with it
Not fearing it

There is no natural order in me
Only humankind creates its illusion

Jacob R. Moses

Card

I found
my grandfather's
business card
in an old black box
of family photos
in our attic.
The once durable
16pt card stock
was badly creased,
its black letters
worn and faded.

The man was a hero
in my mother's eyes.
He died from smoke
and too much whiskey
when I was just a little boy,
so I never got to see
just how great he really was
or really wasn't.

I remember
sitting on his knee
in their Florida room.
It was still dark outside
and the air was filled
with smoke. He was smoking
a Camel cigarette.

He's sometimes in my dreams.
I'm standing over his grave,
weeping. The flat brass gravestone
is covered with Bermuda grass.
It's not been attended to.

I don't know where
the dead go or if it's best
to forget them. I dream
many nights of an empty house
I must wander through, filled
with people I used to know.

Gil Hoy

Snake River Canyon, Idaho

This basket for my dream opened smiling
moments before I saw her husband smile
on my "Lakota death ride."

Even the words she spoke claim
the parallel to words in the dream.
I set death aside—
I knew I'd arrive for my flight home.
I wondered too if that was an eagle we saw,
young and dark, white feathers at the base
of a long narrow tail—yes it was!

This Canyon opening smiling
was shown me as the basket for that dream
a week, ten days before Boise.
Inverted contents.

I met wry Indian guys
who challenged death on our swift steel pony ride,
me curious and solemn to the inside of
the basket where night prevailed
and there was no dying.
A place I am sure was the Canyon at night.
And I walk beside the River, bags on my back,
returning home to my beloved worried about my journey.
Late that Canyon night as I enter our home,
she embraces me, and the dream and the Canyon are one,
and my journey in the basket
prepared by cleansing,
is like the turtles,
this gift from life.

                              Ron Welburn

The Course of Empire Jettisons Its Beginnings
(After a series of paintings by Thomas Cole)

The Course of Empire jettisons its beginnings. The shades of hunters in their skins are locked in forests and then cleared away, gathered into a leafy darkness and felled for the construction of slave ships for the resurrected Eldorado. The hunters move in obscurity to the painter's eye. They live in the stories issued from tradition. We are here, always among them so the dreamers can see us sitting behind the carriage houses and the Greek columns, wearing shabby hats and thick coats. Shell and silver weigh down vessels in the opulent harbor where majesty has the look of something abiding the gestures of decadence, those "over-refinements of style," Al Murray called them, which lure settlements ever away from the spirit of the land. And we return clothed to tribal arts, mingling along distant promontories above the stench and the burning edifice of this glamourous vulture empire, waiting, singing at the drum in our cleansed places.

Ron Welburn

Generations have trod, have trod, have trod*

and I am shackled to the backlit screen,
subjected to technology's caprice,
my feet immobile, hidden, and benumbed,
my thoughts dispelled by cumbrous messages
of discounts, password problems, and a troll,
and so I scroll my Twitter notices
and scan What's Happening, then Google God,
procrastinating still, and find, alas,
my spirit drifts away, mere haze, but then
the images of light dividing clouds
are how we see the brightest wings and warmth,
and you appear and take me by my hand
to share the garden, smell the sweetbush, hear
the cactus wrens, then trill for butterflies.

Luanne Castle

*from the Gerard Manley Hopkins poem, "God's Grandeur"

from "October Sequence"

#54

Artistic evidence of clobbered weeds
Translates to hope discernment will contage
Toward rapid idea generation
Free played in the room in bloom
The wit light crosses practice and dimension
Behold the butterflies at mid-face
Level spaced alert within the trail site
Blemishes go soft thought lifts
The sacrifice imbues needed rest
With fuel via the unexpected
Rise of small nests
Vibratory and distended
After shorn plain spaces prep the evolution
Pure unplanned cyclic as daisies
Admired from the road and glowing
With a honeyed sunlight
Reverberating in slight shadow
Marked by stowaways in thought
As legible as quiet reeds

Sheila E. Murphy

Toxicity

I envy his hollow success.
In every photo he is smiling.
If he is dank and lonely inside,
he hides it well.

His apples are red.
He sold them to the witch
who sold them to Snow White
who took only one bite because the
flesh was mealy and soft.

My apples are irregular and dumpy,
sweet and as flavorful as a
woman perfumed in strawberry wine.

Still, I want his life.
Want to rot inside while
my outsides shine.

Jaya Avendel

The Fairy Ring

The rain has fallen
days on end
moist, misty days
steamy damp nights.

The mushrooms grow
in profusion
a very large fairy ring
for me to dance within,
lit by milky moonlight
shining hazy
in the late-night mists.

The fairies' spell of enchantment
lies heavily on me
as I walk in the daylight,
amazed by rainbows
reflecting in others' glances,
seeming to gather those few
who hear the piper's tune.

We know each other
in an instant's glance.
A gentle smile,
kinship shared in the fairies' ball—
ever dancing in the fairies' ring.

Judy Young

A Chance Encounter

You have a paunch
and breasts like a woman.
Your eyes are flat tires
and years of cheap booze
flush neon veins
in your face.

Vanity eludes us.
We wear our skins
like old coats; parry,
evade the past,
talking about kids,
jobs, and wives,
ignoring the years
we carry around
like twenty extra pounds.

We shared a girlfriend
once —
took turns with her
plumpness
on cool summer nights.

Now, our past sits
like a beggar with cupped hands
while we avert our eyes
and stare into the space
beyond each other's shoulder.

                              Russell duPont

Segregated Cremation

Julie said she wanted me at her cremation
as nonchalantly as she might have asked
to borrow a pen in high school, and I expected
to attend twenty years from now.
But, as a former heavy smoker,
she suffered pneumonia and died in March.

When I read the e-mail on April first, I thought
her normally compassionate partner had made
a tasteless joke.

I Uber to Rosehill Cemetery.
A few family and friends cluster like
the purple irises Julie used to grow.
Unsure who to join, I'm relieved
when Julie's partner beckons me to his car
where we hold hands and reminisce
on the drive to the crematorium.
As usual, we seem unaware of any
racial differences between us.

I note that we settle into pews like
Sunday Church Goers. Whites sit on one side
of the aisle and Blacks on the other,
family and school friends separated
from neighbors and colleagues. Now,
I hold the white hand of Julie's ex-husband.

Several mourners contribute to the eulogy:
how Julie was third in our high school class,
what a kind sister she was and that she was
an inspiring magnet school principal.

I relate an incident from high school, how Julie
covered her geometry test with her hand
when I tried to copy her analysis of angles and squares.
Everyone laughs. I am the last speaker
before the casket rolls through the small metal doors.

Jan Ball

The Story of Us

Twisted upon the realization
that this could be the end,
the ribbon of a subplot
running through the background
pulled suddenly taut as a noose,
catching the casual reader unaware,
the astute in mortal danger
at the turn of a page,
withdrawing across the fold
to make sense of these developments,
removing bifocaled lenses
to rub eyes clear,
wipe a sweaty brow.

How do you unravel
what has taken
300 pages to weave?
How do you defend yourself
from your best friend
stalking with the blade,
advancing from the binding
while you search the paragraphs
for another way?
Why can't this be
a happy ending?

A page turns
then another,
shock numbs into
denial on through
resignation
that escape has not been written
into these final sheets of paper,

only a moment allowed
to find peace in the inevitable,
to hurl curses at the writer
as the binding groans
and the cover slams our story
closed.

Michael E. Strosahl

Figs

Last spring's rain pounded
the earth—riverine flows
danced over iron-red
soil

while hydrangeas chanted
praises. And mild temps

made lilies and asters
saunter upwards. July
slid in, and the fig tree was
cloaked

in scent like a bottle of
Joy perfume left unstoppered.

The palmate leaves hummed and
quickly assembled hundreds
of purple-dressed fruit. They
dropped

off sticky stems. Pods of
living jam, they were too

sweet, too many—small orbs
of candy flesh splitting
skins two sizes too
small,

like jeans bought at eighteen.
I, too, have ripened.

                              Gary Grossman

Ekphrasis

I entered a room I had been in before—
a park beyond, acres of green felt
guarded by fine mesh. I sat
on a cinnabar sofa and was served an orange,
peeled for me by a beautiful woman in whose lap
I, a dragon, had elected to lie.
Afterward, I rose to find, in a gilt frame,
a small oil painting that depicted the very room,
the very room, couch, orange, a Luna moth
glowing turquoise, a gift from a lover,
mounted in a walnut shadow box.
Its wings were pinned with little chance
to catch the wind. Above the sofa,
a small oil painting in a gilt frame.

Bruce Ducker

On Monster.com

I was at work, cruising the web, when my eye stuck on the ad.
Until then, I was window-shopping résumés and jobs, but
this screen ended my search.

BE A CLOUD? NO EXPERIENCE NEEDED.
MUST ENJOY TRAVEL AND THE OUTDOORS.
NO BROKERS OR ACROPHOBES.

I interviewed and was hired, I guess for my sincerity.
When I asked, *But where is the monster?,* they said, *You'll see.*
The probationary period went without a hitch. Mostly
gliding, drifting, scudding. Weather formations. The perils
of condensation. After ground school, I was sent aloft.
Early assignments were easy, cyclonic, counter-cyclonic.

In this line,
one's career soon forks: stratus—the pea soup legion—or cirrus,
suspended and crystalline. The blue skies. The chance to soar.
The cottony stuff that one associates with balmy days,
Polonius, green hillsides. That was for me: I found my calling.
On the lookout for lovers lying in shade, themselves watching for me,
I composed myself into a whale, complete with spindrift spout.
She pointed me out, nudging him from a doze
on her lap to view me. He dreaming of building her a castle
of song. And as he rose on an elbow, shading his eyes
with the book of poems he had brought to read her, I morphed
into a dragon, virga streaming from fleecy nostrils.

My first anniversary review was quite positive,
accompanied by a substantial raise.

Bruce Ducker

The Dead Visit

in our gestures, jokes, intonation
microbes, epidermis, ailments, talents
they linger in a bottle of Estee Lauder *parfum,*
yellow and crumble on Polaroid and Kodachrome

in our DNA, tales of pogroms, poverty,
floods, and famine twist and ascend
to populate our dreams, our worries
visit our seders with Elijah, the Prophet

we're taught to remember the dead
by lighting candles,
saying Kaddish,
giving charity in their memory,
we say *may they rest in peace,*
but they don't—
the dead choose their own way
to remember us

Lois Baer Barr

Honey Locust Trees

pods,
like ribbons
of mourners, hang
    on barren limbs
        north winds send
            boomerangs crackling,
                rattling, snapping,
                curlicued commas scattered
                    upon our streets, our lawns
                        nature, crafty mother,
                            procreates with her
                            resilient, redundant
                            coffee-colored shafts
                        to be unsheathed,
                        to spread seeds
                    in holes where skunks
                    have dug for grubs,
                brown scarabs burrow
            beneath the earth,
        germinate to seedlings,
        saplings, trees
we won't have
breath enough
    to see.

Lois Baer Barr

For Georgia

When I saw you,
it was clear light and
traces of life in
your eyes were doing
a lone vestigial dance
to a joyless music
no longer being heard.

Still, I bought you a drink.

You were never pretty,
you often said, yet
wouldn't let me disagree.
A failed marriage
was followed by a more
permanent one to pills,
booze, and finally heroin.
By the time we met,
death was shadowing
your steps like a
malevolent mime.

I think of you while
watching *It's a Wonderful
Life,* where Jimmy Stewart
rises above the dark tones
of Frank Capra's Americana,
is reborn under an Angel's wings
till thoughts of his failed suicide
vanish like roses in winter.

All of us saw
death in your shadow.

Georgia, you never
were given that worthy gift
of perspective to change.

Found dead on a floor
of an overdose at thirty-six,
your two young children
left behind like shrapnel
on an unnamed battlefield.

And there is little else
as I drink eggnog with whiskey
and watch Jimmy Stewart smile
in a different world that needs
not the subzero winds outside
to chill us to the bone.

Rp Verlaine

Lazarus Act

I can see that you landed
on your feet, even after
the seizures shook you
and they wired your head
to machines that recorded
the ebb and flow of your
electrical misfires.

Your children gathered 'round you,
hunkered down and made plans
for your return
to the world of lucidity.

I watched you
slowly rise up
closer to the surface each day,
as I sat beside your bed
reading you the journals
that mapped our adventures
together. I wanted to knit
the memories into
your consciousness,
call for you over the static,
have you hear me loud
and clear.

The day you woke up crying
because you hadn't died
was the turning point for us.
We stood around your bed smiling
at the beauty of your Lazarus act,
the way you finally turned your head
and listened.

Mary Sexson

Confused Emperor

You are keenly aware
of the disturbances in the field
of your perception.

You hear labored breathing,
music playing,
pool balls clicking
at the eight-ball strike.

You send us into the hallways
of the hospital
to seek out the offenders
as your heightened senses
grab hold and rule, like
a confused emperor who orders
his troops unwittingly
into battle.

Alas,
this is a war you will not win.
The rogue glial cells
in your brain will eventually
take over the topography
of what was once *you*,
rendering you a sovereign nation
of one, closed off
from all that must be understood
in order to thrive
among your loved ones.

Even now
we are letting go, accepting
the tiredness that defines your days,
the unsteady walk that demands a cane,
your beautiful hair almost gone.

Mary Sexson

Magpies, Mythologies, and Celestial Musings

The sun batiks the table
this second September Sunday
as four poets meditate
at the coffeehouse courtyard
to muse over our new poems.
Sparrows eavesdrop as they hop
beneath our table.

Jeff has a trademark on magpies.
He may be a subconscious love poet,
but he's a poet of peace, more so
than George's post-Newtonian
theory poems. Bees dance around my head,
enhance the musicality of Jeff's
"Serenade of the Tibetan Songbird."

A monarch floats along, its reflection
bright in windowpanes. Mike's Aloha
Shirt Man makes a reappearance,
reincarnated as a trickster who writes
his lies to reborn gods. Maybe he wants
to confuse the reader.
I see it as good karma—
no ambulance or fire sirens roaring by.

Bikini girl strolls past, sunglasses larger
than the cloth covering her runway body.
Jim's poem, a well-crafted Midrash,
battles between the wits and wills of gods.
A prophet's line. A trojan horse. We wonder
about the first prankster. Surely Satan.
Good articulation, good alliteration, gets our attention.

"Colts drop home opener" interrupts
our catholic conversation. Over 2000 years
ago we'd be watching the lions
against Christians. Mythology of Cetus.

What knowledge is worth knowing ...
Can you ever know enough ...
who gets to decide?

That's a poem I'd like to spend
more time with ... deep celestial musings.
The girl in the bikini walks toward Mike
with the wink of a whale. Jim's Panama hat—
an obvious knockoff—
scares her away.

Lylanne Musselman

How I Think

Most evenings,
I follow the same path along the grassy patch
when I go out to walk.
I pass the ash oak tree standing tall by the fork of the road.
I know it so well now.
Its ashen and reflecting white and taupe daubed over its bark,
flowing upward along the thinning stems.

Where the lane ends at the intersection and yields to a pompous avenue,
out of habit, I slow down to let pass a lone car
that might emerge unannounced from behind the red maple.
I then turn westward
and my feet pick speed, get nimbler
as I follow the course of the descending sky.
This rhythm I have earned in time.

Yet something changes every day—
the sky more grey than last evening,
a deeper yellow or a lighter blue, perhaps,
from the Friday before.
The blue jays cackle more cheerfully
than the last time I saw a couple perched
on the oak's lower branch.
I notice different details each time
as my legs carry with them the day's experiences—
bits of joys, delights, aches, and discoveries:

I recall an office hour conversation
with a student proving hard
that the characters in the story we read
live in an unfair world much like us.
I mull over my cousin's recipe idea
exchanged over a phone call,
of turning kale-tofu to a delectable American version of saag-paneer.
An email that's waiting to be written, CNN breaking news,
my neighbor's leaky faucet, a nuisance in her kitchen.
Thoughts chaperone me as I walk.

My steps fidgety today, lithe tomorrow.
It depends also on how I read your message.
One day, wrapped in the warmth of meanings
I draw from your note,
I inhale the wafting breeze
and discover a new line of trees, more veins on the leaves,
symmetries that I had not seen the day before.
The blue of the sky suddenly merging
with blazing red and amber.

On another,
the scent in the air leaves me gasping—
shrouded in tragic interpretations of what you wrote,
what you may have actually meant.
The trunk of an ancient elm tree
that I had come to revere so much
looks rugged and stern like never before.
The sky's patient, the path dreary.
I trudge back home, my soul in rags.

It's not about the evenings, or the skies, trees, or the blue jays.
It is not even about you.
It's how I think.

Mahasweta Baxipatra

The Pastel Scarf

She saved her pin money—
pennies, nickels, and dimes, quarters, and the occasional
dollar bill—over a long gray winter,
stashed in that old candy tin, waiting patiently
to purchase a small luxury to welcome spring.
Something bright to wear for Easter.
Something worth every penny.

She found it, the perfect scarf,
at Meyer & Franks ladies' counter, swirling softly
among the crisp white gloves and thick leather handbags.
Its raggedly abstract pastel colors dancing
on the translucent white silk looked to her
like flowers and butterflies, and the drifting ends
made her smile as she whirled it around
her crown of strawberry hair.
It was worth every penny.

She gave it to her grown daughter
on a warm summer birthday, a hand-me-down gift,
a remembrance of child's play,
when her daughter had traipsed about the house
trailing the silken scarf, playing dress-up.
The scarf is now a little worn, now a little faded,
its translucent white now gray with age
like her hair, the brightly colored pastels
like flowers and butterflies now a little softer.
The treasured scarf still made her smile,
and a tear fell when she saw her daughter's eyes light up with joy
as she lifted the silky folds from the tissue,
remembering childhood moments
so clear, this scarf so cherished.
It was worth every penny.

It lies now across a child's pillow,
the drifting ends gently spread, wrapped
around her small head as she sleeps, her breath a little ragged.

The abstract pastel colors still look like flowers
and butterflies dancing upon the translucent white silk,
like her skin, tinged with the grayness of illness, of treatments.
Alone, she wages this war within. Alone, she withstands stares
and whispers as her crown of strawberry hair
is lost in this battle.

The day the last lock fell,
her mother gave her a small tissue-wrapped gift,
a hand-me-down, a remembrance of child's play,
of traipsing about the house trailing the silken scarf,
playing dress-up—now more worn, now more faded,
now even softer, and her eyes lit up as she lifted
the silky folds of her grandmother's pastel scarf.
The flowers and butterflies danced proudly,
and she smiled.

It was worth every penny.

                              Alys Caviness-Gober

Prestige

If I strike my saw
against her chains,
sending out two
perfect golden ringing notes,

then put her
into the painted box,
Sun, Stars, Moon,
until she is mostly
gone,

then cut,
stroke by stroke,
until one
becomes two,

then bow and exit,
there is no magic.

Nobody has prested any digitation.

Mundane is not arcane
until she is revealed,
whole and unharmed,
free
to go or stay
as she pleases.

Chris Hasara

Is it Magic?

Is it magic if
I am delighted by
the found quarter
plucked from the void
behind the ear,
Even though I know it was
in hand
the entire time?

Is it magic if
the dancer moves with
preternatural agility,
Even though I know that years
of study built the
enabling muscles?

Is it magic if,
Even though I know
sunlight produces vitamin D,
I still wait to bask
in the glow of the sun
when the first
morning rays
cut sharp shadows
out of long winter nights?

Let it be magic,
The unexpected delight of
A bird released from a hidden pocket,
A crocus in snow,
Joy in a pain-filled world.

Chris Hasara

Circe on Campus

Circe, the Classical Studies scholar, selects her own sorority.
She turns her frat rat suitors into sisters, then invites them to dine.
The vestiges of men taint this dinner party. Loutish
manners remain. These *nouveau femmes* transform the feast
into a testosteronated banquet by lifting their chair legs,
holding their knives as antlers, and acting as rutting rams
clashing over the centerpiece. At the football stadium,
docile jocks assemble where the jealous Circe has arranged
their transformation into swine. At the fifty-yard line,
they count off their fate, where one in twenty become boars,
the rest, sows. How else to propagate the species of pork chops,
pickled snouts, and tenderloins for the guests at Circe's table?
In the kitchen, Circe's male professors are now aproned-clad women,
seasoning their arguments with scallions and garlic. Brothing
at the mouth, the cooks whip their pigtails till they interlock,
impeding civil intercourse, interrupting the serving of soup.
In the dining hall, Circe sits at the table's head,
    swilling her blood-red wine.

JL Kato

Kicking My Own Ass

No reason to pout and feel sorry for myself,
yet sitting on the couch with the remote, I barely follow the show.
Got a pantry loaded with healthy foods that bring me joy,
while all some folks have comes from the town pantry.
Husky fur on my clothes reminds me I am safe and loved,
enjoying a time of wellness denied to many.

So now, sitting in the quiet, a memory comes to me
of my internship in South Bend with Suzie P.
Checking on her "people" on the potholed streets,
we found a young woman tidying up her corner
in the shadowy parking garage.
I flashed back to the warm bed I left that morning at the Convent,
not aware my journey would take this humble road
Our girl, fresh from a provided breakfast and place to freshen up,
assured us she was up next for housing,
was safe in the shadows of that dirty garage.
Clean clothes folded and hair combed,
she grasped bits that reminded her she was woman of value
even after months on the street.

Humbled by my self-doubts—
a conditioned response from my first thirty trips around the sun—
I took on a new resolve.
No longer can I waste time.
My book may never be written, but my poetry will tell my story.
Home projects will be finished without going into debt.
I will humbly embrace what brings me joy,
share joy where none is found, and
plant seeds from humble roots and lessons learned.
After all, I just want to be remembered for my Gołąbki.

KJ Carter

Cloutie Tree

an ill-advised limbo under a willow branch
and tumble over mossy stone
will force you on your knees
before the cloutie tree.
ankle bone squeezed
between black-mooned nails,
your cries won't ring out as they should.
supplication will be whispered awhile,
slinking off into mulch.

damp ferns tremble at this ancient well
where songbirds wait, confused
at an ill-defined task.
a plastic minion peers out
from under his leafy quilt,
put to bed but not to sleep.
sky keeps itself drawn over a wound,
and through the gloom,
headlights blink obscenity.

do you know if melodies will return
to rouse tartan ribbons in May,
if fibres will exhale their fractures,
if a baby's dummy caught on string
will whirl, faster and faster,
like a wonky swing before the cry
of joyful unfurling, and bluebells,
sprung from things that never quite fit
will pass, through rot, into light?

Will Griffith

The Traveler

School looms in the August of our days.
Cleaning closets, trying on last year's jeans
stirs memories.
As I entered, the pain of the day waited.
My sorrow is becoming like a used comforter.
Each time I pull it up around my shoulders, it seems new.
I sat on the floor of our bedroom and looked at slides
from our early days, our apartment days,
days of loving and making love.
I see his handsome face, handsome chest.
I so want to hold him, touch him.
Knowing, knowing, knowing this is not productive.
I notice in the picture hanging around his neck—
the Saint Christopher medal
lost long before his passing.
The suffocating pain was too much.
Happy to have these photos of him,
I tucked them away for another day.
Turning around in my disheveled bedroom,
on top of my clothes, papers, and pile of hangers
I saw the Saint Christopher medal.
I cannot know where it has been,
Or know how it came to be.
I clutched the chain, thanking God for my gift.

Jan Hall

Discovering Home

We crossed Sugar Creek and Horseshoe Bend
on a cool spring day we stole from time.
We rested in a plowed field,
continued on through overgrown weeds and trees,
climbed a fence or two, and
came upon the hidden cabin.
The doors were open.

All around the cottage, lilacs were budding.
We went in and were greeted by friendly spirits.
We pictured a wagon coming in the front circle drive
with a farmer and his young bride.
In the wagon, they would have carried her piano.
Her music would have serenaded the old Indian burial mound.

One October day, decades later,
I drove down the bumpy gravel road
and met some hunters parked in the drive.
They said there was indeed a cute little house back there.
I left with the owner's name and the knowledge I would return.
I went back on a day in May, another day stolen from time.

When I ended up at the spot, it was expecting me.
Over every hill, under every oak
were lovely lavender wildflowers—
the Appendaged Waterleaf picked that day to bloom.
I startled bluebirds in the brush.
The sun shone through, and the path led back.

Jim said, "I made spring more than green
that day we walked to Horseshoe Bend."
Perhaps Jim and I shared another lifetime in that cabin,
or maybe I was one of the last Miami to be buried there.
These secrets I cannot know,
yet do know that the road to the little house leads me home.

Jan Hall

Inner City Birdlife

There were no nightingales,
but something much stranger
came to Mutley Plain
that September night

Not the roar of a goal
reverberating round
cement back yards
from satellite screens
of an all-day pub

Not the couples carrying
their Friday feasts,
bringing back the korma
and beer
(swilled down with a big row
overheard by all and sundry)

Not the students in their chicken houses
spilling out, all mess and make-up,
hormones akimbo,
squatting in suburban roads,
front rooms full of traffic cones,
reliquaries to bad taste

But as we leant over
the ash and clinker
prodding the dying bbq,
a Barn Owl sitting on a pole
turned his head and stared at the
strange indoor-outdoor habitat,
neither one thing
nor the other

Jacky Pugh

Hymn to Vitiligo

Dappled skin is my superpower.
I walk in curtains of shade
white symmetry of knees, hands, feet
reveals to those in the know
a changeling on the turn
long past the growing years.

What to fear?
Not specific danger
but diffuse blending colour.
Uncertainty.
There is magic in this reverse leopard.
Whether for good or evil, I signal
something with my witchy skin.
Mark my words.

Jacky Pugh

Haunts and Houses

On a trip home from Florida,
I visited a house my grandparents had lived in
that had been almost half consumed by fire.
Roof completely gone,
soot and charring over one end,
framing and broken windows sticking out
like jagged bones,
sitting there with the rain falling in.

It was a gorgeous house:
red brick,
white trim,
big expanse of cushiony green grass.
A two-story with a full basement,
each level had been converted into
its own three-bedroom living space.
They, however, lived there alone.
Mostly.

This house was haunted.
I've lived with friendly ghosts
in more than one place;
I didn't live here but visited daily.

More than once,
we heard someone pick up the receiver
of the wall phone in the kitchen,
dial it, and let it ring.
We were sitting at the table beside the phone.
No one was there.

From the main level,
we'd hear lots of people walking around upstairs.
We'd hear the outside door to the landing open and close,
and the door to that level open and close,

footsteps on the stairs
while the party was in play.
They sounded like a very social group.

The ghosts in the basement
were quieter and less active.
We would only occasionally
hear doors open and close—
sometimes when we were upstairs,
sometimes when we were in the basement.

My grandfather was a very heavy man.
I was practicing the piano one day
and thought I heard him walking behind me.
No one was there.

They weren't a problem. They just *were*.

Standing, looking at the burnt house,
I wondered if those ghosts were still there
and felt some sadness
that they, also,
might have lost their home.

Marilyn J Wolf

Etive Inversion

Waked at last,
to spring's bright shimmering dawn,
effort, cold and broken sleep
forgotten now,
for as I slept,
cold air crept,
furtive from the rugged west,
and drowned lush Etive
in a sea of cloud.
And in that new day's golden light,
from my quiet windless height,
grey peaks sailed
like ships afloat a calm slate sea.

Martin Goldie

White Flag

Its chalky whiteness
ghostly in the summer murk,
a beacon in the gloom,
that humble linen
tied atop a weathered picket,
that makeshift flag
sad symbol of surrender,
blowing softly in that summer's
gentle breeze
on the edge of this land's
grey eternal seas.
Alone, it danced an aching waltz,
beyond a field of cotton grass,
swaying slowly in the wind
among the baking machair's
muted flowers,
above that busy beach
of ashen sand.

Martin Goldie

The Host

Trickster hosts an open mike
once a week in Chicago.

One night I'm there,
excited to be out
and anxious to read a new poem.

Trickster tells me I'll read last.

In time, he says,
"... and next, our last poet tonight.
But first,
let me read my new piece ..."

And he reads my poem.

Jeffrey Spahr-Summers

doux rêve, doux chien

My elderly dog is soft & tired, gold & small & white-headed, dark
Thick pads on his paws. His final few puffing pants, I pray

Will not seize. He'll muse friendily on funny little ants, some
Whuffy desert dust, a rare blue spider: a dream or desire.

One huge red cucaracha with horrifying antennae that ventures on
To his body when he's just lying around, assuming the world.

Maybe he'll muse on me. Maybe he'll muse on our Kona-side beach
Flaps, the seahorse lab: his obsession with the rubber hamburger. I

Hope. Is Kamali's death, a moment that has not taken place,
About him? Is his death about this world? Is his death a testament

To stars? Water in a bottomless bowl? A waterless bowl?
Is Kamali's death about the satellite I think we see in the sky

In the one morning hour the two of us wander together, staring at
Grass, musing stupidly like two stalling speedboats, carousing

Like clowns? Or is K's death about plants? Sniffy plants. O black
& ginger plants. Trampled plants, sister plants.

Plants with tendril ornaments, canopied stepped-on cigarettes.
Sure, the world's a tangle, though in death, it's all a comfy

Clump. I hope.

Sound's behind, long behind, a silent solo plane in an awfully
Clear blue sky. One concise desert cloud. You know, I'm sixty, & I

Never knew love really worked like this. I'd always thought:
"Monarchs." Man o man, was I wrong about that. Kamali sprawls,

Many months before dying, on the tile, cool, & I wrap myself, a
Hard puppet on the bed: a firefighter, fighting.

Rebecca Byrkit

American Karma
—for J.T.

The reason we'll never understand lives inside
the reason we have to name. It's the same
reason all the maps on my walls
are misdrawn in the same way: with us
disproportionate, at the center,
but a little higher.

High & away, past orbits
& dying stars, past diffuse nebulae
that shame the clouds, that gods look up at
from their backs, there is nothing & it's beautiful.
We are Fate's jackals, the counterpunch.
A swarm of luxuriant ants building what's worse
than useless, what's ugly. A moving portrait
of emptiness.

There's no profit in a library
filled with words worse than lies,
words without meaning. The big donor came inside her
family, fed her gluttonous want. He doesn't come around
anymore. Her hands are full of throbbing ghosts. Sometimes
the best thing you can do for the working parts
is to scrap the car.

Out & away, next to the nothing,
God's son asks, like yours,
for five more minutes
at the batting cage, knowing
the right pitch will come back around.

Kyle Hunter

The High Priestess: II

When he was a child, he was always waiting.
Sometimes he knew what he was waiting for.
& sometimes not.
He could recognize the most basic thing
As a source of anxiety, like a door
On Halloween,
A Christmas present, a thank you letter,
Unopened, unwritten, just waiting there
Like him, the knot
In the diagram in the manual
For the cub scout,
Resembling his throat or his stomach,
As they felt to him. It all made him sick,
All that waiting, for practice to end,
For class to end, for studies to end,
This girl to say yes, that girl to say no,
A wrestling match, an application …
He never knew it took care of itself.
It took a long time to learn how to wait.
He didn't know it was a profession.
But she served him beers at twenty-something
& he waited.
She sold cigarettes. She sold him coffee,
Mornings after.
Each clerk, each waitress, was his high priestess.
He waited on them. They waited on him.
It took a long time to learn how to wait,
But they taught him.
He could have married any one of them
Without waiting.
But he waited for another,
One who did not know what it meant to wait for him
To come around.
She waited some. But it took care of itself,

This thing between them. & he could wait
For the debts or the fever to go down,
For the time to write, or the space. Or
For her to read something very much like this. Or
Finally
Get it.

J. T. Whitehead

Tarot card art by Josh Johnson

Resurrection Poem for My Father

One night, I found myself suddenly
at my father's funeral,
although he had been dead many decades.
He lay in his coffin and others went to look at him,
but I sat, not wanting to see him cold and inert.

Then, unexpectedly, he began to stir.
I thought, "That's impossible! He's already embalmed!
It's a temporary aberration."
But he went on to sit up and climb out of his coffin.
He spoke to someone, his words uncharacteristically kind,
so unlike his previous harshness.

I thought, "It's a miracle, but it won't last."
However, he went on to walk around,
and others seemed to seek his advice,
his words having gathered weight
from his sojourn in a vaster world.

He spoke to me, too, saying seriously,
"Full fetal gravitas,"
like a priest giving a benediction,
as if I should have known what that meant,
words which I still cannot fully fathom,
that hint, perhaps, at living from the depths
of our inborn human dignity.

I brought him a delicate soup,
not knowing what to feed the recently revived.
As far as I knew, Lazarus' first meal
was not recorded.

I grasp my father's resurrection
like a fragile flower,
not knowing how to hold it.
I want to make more of our kinship this time
than either of us could ever do
with its original blossoming.

                                    Mary Kay Turner

In the Dominican

I'm operating on a man
in an impoverished Third World hospital
built sometime in the last century,
when my anesthesiologist states
with deceptive calmness, "I've lost his rhythm."
Indeed, the heart monitor reveals a childish scribble
replacing the previous regular pulsating waves.
The muscular machine of his heart has begun to unwind.

My perception expands to include everything—
the jolting of compressions on the man's chest as we start CPR,
a second set of capable hands joining mine
as we rush to complete what we started.
Voices and bodies offering assistance with palpable goodwill,
while the back of my mind grinds away
with possible diagnoses and treatments,
gnawing concern for his well-being,
the renewal of shock at the fragility of the human form.

An eternity later, the scribble on the monitor
abruptly resumes a steady cadence.
The thumping on the man's sternum ceases.
We finish our urgent stitching,
turn off the anesthetic, and wait.
A long time. And longer and longer yet.
He still does not regain consciousness.
It becomes evident that he will not.
The insult to his brain cannot be remedied.

The yoke of responsibility settles with familiar heaviness
as my feet reluctantly carry my leaden heart
down the cinderblock corridor
to tell the family the terrible news.

Just as I reach the waiting room door,
the nurse pulls me back, crying breathlessly,
"He's waking up!"
I fly back along the corridor to the OR,
where the man, now perfectly alert,
asks us, in puzzled Spanish,
what in the world we have been doing.
Lazarus' companions could not be more astonished.

I take him to the recovery room and try to get an EKG,
but the ancient machine only stands in the corner,
holding up a plant.
The senior surgeon says "Stop. You are trying to make an ICU
out of two bottle caps and a paper clip."
It's true. I stop.
Instead, I can only yield to amazement.

Don't read this poem to the very young,
because I'm going to confess
that, although there is no Santa Claus,
there is a special emissary of God
who makes his sober rounds on those with few resources,
excepting hope—
drunkards, children, mission doctors
and other such ingenuous fools.

                              Mary Kay Turner

The Hill O' Many Stanes

A pantry of organic nettle tea
and skeins of wild raspberries
tumble through the turnstile
between times
of concrete & standing stones
where sky sits
a duck-egg blue ceiling
on the Hill O' Many Stanes

The Land O' The Cat
where hairy-brottachs hatch
into louded yellow and
green-veined white butterflies
and dandelion clocks puff
among mosaics of standing stones

Kneeling at a silver stone-pew
palming ley lines with my lifelines
I am litmus among lichen
waking-dreaming of way-back-when
the Wee Folk jigged
in amethyst heather and Fairy Rings
in The Land O' the Cat
where the veil's still thin between worlds

Mandy Beattie

To Know a River

Start where you would
to know all things,
at its mouth.

Get in moonstruck,
ready to move with the tides.
Float like you're among friends.
Swing back and forth in the wind with the cordgrass.

Leave sunbaked and blossomed,
a pale dressed starfish,
skin a pink sunrise
with the pull of the moon on your bloodstream,

knowing you'll return
next time it's at its closest,
before the cordgrass yellows
and the beaches gather straw,
with salt on your lips.

Jordan Krais

Night Walk

The half-moon smeared
in a milky puddle of cloud,
its light greying the air
with a memory of ghosts.

I'm looking for yours
somewhere in this damp
riverbank wood,
out among the trees,
waiting to fall into step
with me on the yielding
sponge of old leaves.

We'll not need words:
they will all be said
by the separate melodies
of water falling;
we'll not want sight
of each other's faces:
yours will be shaded,
ambiguous as the path,
mine blanked with guilt.

I'll touch your hand once.
It will be warm and alive,
and later remember, below us,
the winter-filled stream,
its constant roar.

                                        Ruth Aylett

The Farmhouse

On the way to Geneseo, it rises out of the mid-August heat
sharp and jagged, gasping for any cool breeze at all.
Once upon a time, life kicked within it, and it held itself
like an expectant mother who smiles each time she touches her stomach.

It stood proud once, freshly painted,
the comforting smells of bread baking within,
an apple pie cooling on the kitchen windowsill,
a dog lying near the back steps, snoozing in the late afternoon sun.

In between the cicadas' rhythms, there were raucous fights and parties,
screaming orgasms with headboards banging,
rain pouring off the roof,
    wind howling and the muffled sounds people make
when they bury a loved one.

Now empty and forgotten, the ivy eats it board by board
greedily engulfing the entire lower floor, stretching its sticky
fingers upstairs, past the shattered windows, the black eyes swollen shut,
the red trim peeling and dark, dried blood caked into its sides.

Its sadness reaches out to me. Or maybe it is just my own sadness
bubbling up after all these years. If the house had arms, it would lurch
across the expanse of highway to grab me as old people do
when you walk down the hallway of a nursing home.

Maybe if I was a different person, I would have gone to the house,
sung it a lullaby, whispered gently as I lit matches near the front door,
respecting it enough to hear its final confession, watch it heave
    its final breath before giving itself over to whomever watches us all.

Instead I continue to drive further and further east,
    wishing I had the chance
to become myself all over again. Because then, I would become
the type of person who would bear witness to something like this,
and remember it always.

Instead of being this person, afraid to make eye
contact, afraid that if I stop, all I will to do is climb up its
uneven stairs and curl up in the farthest corner until the autumn
breeze cools me down.

                                    Lucy J. Madison

You

You.
The word flanking my deepest core,
a beacon in the dark night,
a path weaving its way from the thicket to the oceanside
where waves roll ashore in time with my heartbeat.

You.
The one who annexed my marrow,
a single cell dividing,
a cure plaiting alpha and omega together in me
where separation is only in my mind.

You.
The prayer I speak to the cosmos,
a knowing in my being,
an unfettered certainty, elemental
where evolution meets a single passage.

You.
The love of all my lives condensed,
a lesson and a journey,
a hand reaching out to embrace mine as we begin again,
our footsteps merged in the sand, a memento
until the tide returns.

Lucy J. Madison

Lessons in Magic

People are jaded and hardened by the world.
They say that magic is not real,
but I have seen magic—I have.

Magic is hearing your heartbeat for the first time
and holding your mother's hand and trying not to cry.
It's looking at your shadowy silhouette
and realizing the beauty of this moment,
knowing that my eyes are staring at the product of love
and the answer to prayers.

Magic is feeling you kick for the first time
and waiting for you to do it again,
reading books to you and letting you know that we love you.
It's preparing our home for your arrival,
adorning a room with pink and glitter just for you.

Yes, my sweet daughter, whom I have not yet met,
let me reassure you that magic is real.
I know because you have cast a spell on me.

W. B. Cornwell

The Truth

Weighted blanket pulled up to my chin,
a sense of unease seeped into my bones.
I needed the pressure to calm my worried mind,
and as I breathed slowly into a state of zen,
his voice whispered with gentleness and love,
"Close your eyes and slip into sleep, sweet one.
"Rest. You'll feel better."
I found a peaceful slumber.

But as suddenly as comfort crept across me,
it was ripped away—
the weighted blanket
no longer the only pressure felt.
A sharp pain settled in the depths of my gut.
Gasping for air, I told myself,
"Dissociate. Do not fall into the depths of the dark."

For hours,
my brain was absent from my body,
only coming back
when a familiar sound graced my ears:
a text—such a simple thing to pull me back to reality.
Scrambling for my phone and glancing at the screen,
I realized why I had deeply panicked.
One text from him:
"It's over."
I knew what it meant, and
a million emotions ran through my soul.
It was my right to ask questions.

Kaela Hinton

Haunted by White Nightgowns

The house is haunted by white nightgowns.
Am I the only one who sees them?
The daughter who returned after his death
and watched you stride back and forth
from kitchen to dining to living room
or chasing a dream in the upstairs hallway,
the classic white cotton nightgown
billowing, ghostlike, as your steps quickened.

Sixty-one years is a long time to live with someone
you love, nourish, depend upon, and know so well.
I was a presence in the house, one you seemed to need
at night but found annoying in daylight hours.
I didn't know how to cope with that
after rejecting a challenging job across the world
to witness you wandering throughout the night,
searching for your most cherished memories.

Even as the first year stretched into two, you
couldn't find your place in the big house you
had occupied for more than fifty years
with him and six children, one lost too soon,
then only him for many busy, contented years
of retirement, church, and grandchildren.

Once you joined him in the final journey,
I left the house but still imagine the
white nightgowns, one up and one down
searching for what came before goodbye.

Maureen Brustkern

135

David Allen was born in the South and raised on Long Island. He is a retired journalist with almost four decades on newspapers in New York,  Virginia, and Indiana, and in the Far East, he spent nineteen years reporting for *Stars and Stripes,* the newspaper for the U.S. military community overseas. He is a member of the Last Stanza Poetry Association and the Poetry Society of Indiana, where he served as vice president and contest director. He is also the host of open mic poetry nights in Anderson, IN. David has been published in numerous poetry journals and anthologies and has published four books of poetry, *The Story So Far, (more), Type Dancing,* and *Deadlines Amuse Me.* davidallenpoet.net.

Peter Anderson was born and raised in the suburbs of Detroit and now lives in Vancouver, Canada. His prose poems have appeared in *Unbroken, Sublunary Review, Flora Fiction, Thieving Magpie, Rat's Ass Review,* the *American Journal of Poetry,* and others. His poem "Wobble" in *MoonPark Review* has been nominated for Best Microfictions 2022. His plays are available online at the Canadian Play Outlet.

Michael Ansara spent many years as an activist and an organizer. He is the co-founder of Mass Poetry. He currently serves on the Executive  Committee of the New Movement to Redress Racial Segregation and the organizing team for Together We Elect. His poems and essays have been published in *Salamander, Mid America Poetry Review, Web del Sol, Ibbetson Street, Glint Literary Review, Euphony, Pine Hills Review, Vox, Solstice,* and *Arrowsmith.* His first book of poems, *What Remains,* will be published next summer by Kelsay Press.

Jaya Avendel is a word witch from the Blue Ridge Mountains of Virginia, passionate about life where it intersects with writing and the dreamscapes lost in between. A diversely published writer both online and in print, she shares publication news, creative writing, and writing guides at ninchronicles.com.

Ruth Aylett lives and works in Edinburgh, Scotland. Her poetry is widely published in magazines and anthologies. She has been known to perform with a robot. Her latest pamphlet, *Queen of Infinite Space,* was published by Maytree (maytreepress.co.uk) in late 2021. For more, see macs.hw.ac.uk/~ruth/writing.html

Jan Ball has had 354 poems published in various journals, including: *ABZ, Mid-American Review, Parnassus*, and *Puerto del Sol.* Finishing Line Press published her three chapbooks and first full-length poetry collection, *I Wanted To Dance With My Father. Orbis* nominated her for the Pushcart Prize in 2020. Besides her poetry, Jan wrote a dissertation at the University of Rochester: *Age and Natural Order in Second Language Acquisition.* She was a nun for seven years, then lived in Australia for fourteen years with her Aussie husband and two children. Jan has taught ESL in Rochester, New York, and Loyola and DePaul Universities in Chicago. When not traveling or gardening at their farm, Jan and her husband like to cook for friends.

Lois Baer Barr lives in Riverwoods with her husband and pandemic puppy. The pup loved the rattle and length of honey locust pods. Barr Googled them to make sure they were not toxic and learned enough to write a poem. *LSJ, Rattle*, and *Valley Voices have published her poems* in the past two years. Her interview with Tim Green, editor of *Rattle*, can be seen on YouTube. Her chapbook, *Tracks: Poems on the "El,"* was a finalist at Finishing Line Press and will be published there. She has received three Pushcart Nominations and was a finalist for the Rita Dove Poetry Award.

Marilyn Baszczynski, originally from Ontario, Canada, lives and writes in rural Iowa. Her book, *Gyuri. A Poem of wartime Hungary*, was published in 2015. Her poetry has appeared in the *TelepoemBooth Iowa* art installation and in anthologies and journals including *Abaton, Aurorean, Backchannels, Gyroscope, Healing Muse, KYSO Flash, Loch Raven Review, Midwest Poetry Review, Purifying Wind, Slippery Elm, Tipton Poetry Journal,* and

Whistling Shade. Marilyn is currently Editor of Iowa Poetry Association's annual anthology, *Lyrical Iowa.*

Roderick Bates is the editor of *Rat's Ass Review.* He has published poems in *The Dark Horse, Stillwater Review, Naugatuck River Review, Cultural Weekly, Hobo Camp Review, Asses of Parnassus, Three Line Poetry, Red Eft Review, Ekphrastic Review,* and *Anti-Heroin Chic,* among others. He also writes prose and won an award from the International Regional Magazines Association for an essay published in *Vermont Life.* He is a Dartmouth graduate with a degree in Religion. He lives, writes, and edits in southern Vermont.

Mahasweta Baxipatra lives and teaches in Bloomington, Indiana. Mahasweta writes poems and non-fictional prose and translates fiction from various Indian languages to English. She can be reached at mahabax@gmail.com.

Mandy Beattie's poetry is a tapestry of stories & imagery rooted in people & place, often with an element of other-worldliness. Her poems have been published in: *Poets Republic, Wordpeace, Dreich, Wee Dreich, The Haar, Purple Hermit, Wordgathering, The Clearance Collection, Spilling Cocoa with Martin Amis, Marble Poetry Broadsheet, Book Week Scotland,* & her writing is in The People's Poem of Scotland.

Michelle Blake has published three novels with Putnam Penguin, and essays and poems in *Tin House, Ploughshares, Southern Review, Prairie Schooner, NY Times, Mid-American Review, Solstice, Mezzo Cammin,* and others. She was awarded  publication for her chapbook, *Into the Wide and Startling World,* in the New Women's Voices contest at Finishing Line. She has received residency grants from Vermont Studio Center, Hambidge, and Siena Art Institute; she taught writing at Goddard, Stanford, and Tufts, and was director of the MFA Programs at both Goddard and Warren Wilson College. She has an MFA from Goddard and an MTS from Harvard Divinity School. She currently lives half the year in Mobile, Alabama and the other half in Westminster West, Vermont.

Amy Brewer-Davenport is a lifelong artist who finally made the decision to dedicate everyday to art, nature, and the magic in the forests. You can find this art goblin in the studio, on a road trip, or down by the creek. Much of this art is inspired by folklore, Appalachian wanderings, and beloved books of many types. Find full-color paintings, prints, jewelry, and more at: www.amybdart.com and follow her on Instagram at @amybdart

Michael Brockley is a retired school psychologist who lives in Muncie, Indiana where he is looking for a dog to adopt. His poems have appeared in *Global Poemic, Woolgathering Review,* and *Fatal Flaw.* Poems are forthcoming in *Flying Island* and *The Parliament Literary Magazine.*

Michael H. Brownstein has been widely published throughout the small and literary presses. His work has appeared in *The Café Review, American Letters and Commentary, Skidrow Penthouse, Xavier Review, Hotel Amerika, Free Lunch, Meridian Anthology of Contemporary Poetry, The Pacific Review, Poetrysuperhighway.com* and others. In addition, he has nine poetry chapbooks including *The Shooting Gallery* (Samidat Press, 1987), *Poems from the Body Bag* (Ommation Press, 1988), *A Period of Trees* (Snark Press, 2004), *What Stone Is* (Fractal Edge Press, 2005), *I Was a Teacher Once* (Ten Page Press, 2011) and *Firestorm: A Rendering of Torah* (Camel Saloon Press, 2012). His latest volumes of poetry, *A Slipknot to Somewhere Else* (2018) and *How Do We Create Love?* (2019), were recently released (Cholla Needles Press).

Maureen Brustkern became a poet after retiring from a career as an early educator and a professor of early childhood education in the United States and the Middle East. She recently retired to Indiana to be near her grandchildren and pursues poetry through local and national groups and classes. Her poems have been published in the Carmel Creative Writers' Anthology and Highland Park Poetry.

Rebecca (Becky) Byrkit's poems have appeared in *Ploughshares, The New England Review, Best American Poetry, Arizona Highways,*

Crazyhorse, Sonora Review, Black Warrior Review, the *Best of Exquisite Corpse,* and elsewhere. She lives and teaches in Arizona.

Dan Carpenter is a freelance writer and former Indy Star columnist, born and residing in Indianapolis. His poems have appeared in *Last Stanza Poetry Journal, Poetry East, Pearl, Xavier Review, Southern Indiana Review,* and other journals. He has published two books of poems, *The Art He'd Sell for Love* (Cherry Grove) and *More Than I Could See* (Restoration).

Kathy Jo (KJ) Carter, Urban Dirt Devil, is Indiana to the core, descended from Welsh farmers and Russian/Prussian ethnicity. Retired nurse, musician, and great-grandmother, this mystery buff found a niche in poetry and prose. Who knew? Published in *Indiana Voice Journal, Poets of Madison County, Ink to Paper,* the Poetry Society of Indiana anthology, and  *Last Stanza* Journals. Mystery in the works! Kathy is a member of Last Stanza Poetry Society.

Alys Caviness-Gober is an anthropologist, artist, and writer. Despite lifelong disabilities, Alys perseveres with art and nonprofit volunteering. She comes late to the life of a professional artist; after receiving her MA  in Anthropology, Alys taught Anthropology and Women's Studies at the collegiate level for several years and was a PhD candidate in Applied Linguistics until her disabilities worsened. Alys serves on the Noblesville Cultural Arts Council and is active in the local arts scene. She is the co-founder of NICE (Noblesville Interdisciplinary Creativity Expo); in 2018 NICE received an Indiana Humanities project grant. In November of 2014, she founded Logan Street Sanctuary, Inc. (LSS), an all-volunteer 501(c)(3) arts organization providing the community with diverse arts projects and programming. In July 2019, LSS rebranded as Community • Education • Arts, Inc. (CEArts), continuing many of LSS' annual place-making projects and expanding with digital content. Alys is editor of CEArts' annual submissions-driven anthology, *The Polk Street Review,* Alys' artwork, photographs, and poetry have received national and international recognition.

Luanne Castle's *Kin Types,* a chapbook of poetry and flash, was finalist for the Eric Hoffer Award. Her first collection of poetry, *Doll God,* won the New Mexico-Arizona Book Award for Poetry. Luanne has been a Fellow at the Center for Ideas and Society at the University of California, Riverside. She studied at University of California, Riverside (PhD); Western Michigan University (MFA); and Stanford University. Her Pushcart and Best of the Net-nominated poetry and prose have appeared in *Copper Nickel, American Journal of Poetry, Pleiades, River Teeth, TAB, Verse Daily, Glass: A Journal of Poetry, Broad Street,* and other journals.

Jan Chronister is the author of five chapbooks and two full-length collections of poetry. After serving as president of the Wisconsin Fellowship of Poets for six years, she is stepping down and hopes to have more time to spend on her writing and gardens, including Queen Rhubarb.

W.B. Cornwell is an award-winning poet, novelist, genealogy blogger, and half of the writing team known as Storm Sandlin. Since 2014, he has been published in over a dozen books. He is a member of Last Stanza Poetry Association. In 2016, Ben and his cousin A.N. Williams organized the campaign for Elwood, Indiana's Poetry Month. He is a featured writer for Goodkin.org and is currently working on a slew of writing projects, including various charity publications, co-authorships, and screenplays.

Say Davenport grew up running through the woods, finding magic in absolutely everything. At University, she studied cultures and religion because she's fascinated by the world and what people find in it that makes it have meaning for them. She is a writer, educator, big dog lover, and avid traveler who seeks adventure wherever she can, either out in the world or between the pages  of a book. As a writer, she takes inspiration from the idea that a person should write what they want to read and, for her, that usually means magic and salt.

Bruce Ducker's numerous poems and stories have been published in leading journals, including in *The New Republic; the Yale, Southern, Sewanee, Literary, American Literary, Missouri,* and *Hudson Reviews; Shenandoah; Commonweal; the New York Quarterly; the PEN/America Journal;* and *Poetry Magazine.* The prize-winning author of eight novels and a book of short fictions, he lives in Colorado.

Russell Dupont is the author of two novels: *King & Train* and *Waiting for the Turk.* He is also the author of four chapbooks: *Up in Wisconsin: Travels with Kinsley; There is No Dam Now at Richford;* and two books of poetry: *Winter, 1948* and *Establishing Home Plate.* His poetry has been published in various literary magazines, including *The Albatross, The Anthology of South Shore Poets, Oddball, Adelaide, Rye Whiskey Review* and *JerryJazzMusician.* His story, "The Corner," appears in the anthology *Streets of Echoes.* His journalism has appeared in *The Dorchester Community News, The Melrose Free Press* and *The Patriot Ledger.* He is also a photographer, painter, and printmaker whose works have been widely exhibited and are in public and private collections.

Martin Goldie lives with his wife Janice and their dogs in the village of Ardentinny, Argyll, Scotland. He enjoys reading and listening to music and has been writing poetry for just over a year. Since childhood, he has loved hill walking, and many of his poems are inspired by landscape, the weather which influences our experience of the land, and the flora and fauna which colour our wild and white places.

James Green is a retired university professor and administrator. He has published four chapbooks of poetry and a fifth, titled *Ode to El Camino de Santiago and Other Poems of Journey*, is forthcoming from Finishing Line Press. His individual poems have appeared in literary journals in Ireland, the UK, and the USA. His website can be found at www.jamesgreenpoetry.net

Will Griffith is a poet from Cornwall who teaches philosophy in a Secondary School. He has had work published online and in print and is working on his first collection.

John D. Groppe, Professor Emeritus at Saint Joseph's College,  Rensselaer, IN, has published in *Tipton Poetry Journal, Flying Island, From the Edge of the Prairie, Christianity Today, The National Catholic Reporter,* and other journals. His poem "A Prophet Came to Town" was nominated for a Pushcart Prize (2013). His poem "Sudden Death" won honorable mention in Embers poetry contest (1984). His poetry collection *The Raid of the Grackles and Other Poems* (Iroquois River Press) was published in 2016. He is listed on the Indiana Bicentennial Literary Map 200 Years: 200 Writers.

Gary Grossman is a Professor of Animal Ecology at the University of Georgia. He enjoys poetry, running, fishing, gardening, songwriting, and singing as well as sculpting. He is a father of two daughters and married to a newly retired professor of nutrition. Poetry credits include *Verse-Virtual, Pearl, Trouvaille Review, Last Stanza Poetry Journal, Poetry Life and Times,* and a *Poetry Motel* broadside. Gary is currently working on fictional memoirs in both graphical and text formats.

Janet Cox Hall writes: When I was sixteen in my American Literature class, I discovered poetry. Thanatopsis had a picture of a man standing  overlooking a gorge. When I climbed trail thirteen at Turkey Run and looked over the valley, I thought I was William Cullen Bryant. Of course, walking up there I saw "two roads diverged in the woods." Nature and words spoke to me then and now. I have lived in an A-frame on Morse Reservoir for fifty years this fall. In this spot I have raised three children, dogs, and now a cat. I retired from teaching elementary school in 2012. Now I raise flowers and pay lumberjacks to cut down my dead trees. I failed to mention I am a Hoosier by birth, but a Boilermaker by the grace of God.

Chris Hasara is a father of four and husband of one in Northern Indiana. He studied creative writing at Western Kentucky University and has applied that education to a successful career as a truck driver and farmer. His words have appeared in *From the Edge of the Prairie,* recent volumes of *The Last Stanza Poetry Journal,* and volume 6 of the Poetry Society of Indiana book *Ink to Paper*.

Elizabeth Hill is a retired lawyer living in Harlem with her husband and two irascible cats. She was an Administrative Law Judge deciding suits between learning disabled children and the school system. She grew up in New Hampshire and on Cape Cod. Elizabeth is an avid walker and enjoys Pilates. Her work has been/is soon to be published in *34th Parallel Magazine, Blue Lake Review, Blue Moon Art & Literary Review,* and *Calliope*.

John R. Hinton is an Indiana poet and writer. His writing is inspired by our daily human interactions and the accompanying emotions: love, hate,  indifference, passion. His words explore who we are, how we behave. Sometimes eloquent, other times gritty, these words seek to reveal the joy and pain of living this beautiful human existence. He is the author of two poetry collections: *Blackbird Songs* and *Held.* John is the Vice President of the Poetry Society of Indiana and a member of Last Stanza Poetry Association.

Kaela Hinton is an aspiring poet from Indiana writing about the deep emotions that come from living life and experiencing the world around her. She currently works with children who are on the autism spectrum, and also frequently dabbles in the culinary field.

Gil Hoy is a widely published Boston poet and writer who studied poetry and writing at Boston University through its Evergreen program. Hoy previously received a B.A. in Philosophy and Political Science from Boston University, an M.A. in Government from Georgetown University, and a J.D. from the University of Virginia School of Law. Hoy is a semi-retired trial lawyer. His work has recently appeared in *Best Poetry Online, Muddy River Poetry Review, The Galway Review, Tipton Poetry Journal, Rusty Truck, Mobius: The Journal of Social Change, The*

Penmen Review, Misfit Magazine, Rat's Ass Review, Chiron Review, The New Verse News, and elsewhere. Hoy was nominated for a *Best of the Net* award last year.

Kyle Hunter's poems have appeared in *Main Street Rag, Rockvale Review, So It Goes, Gravel,* and elsewhere. His work in *Flying Island* was recently nominated for the Best of Net Anthology. When he's not writing or wrangling his five young kids, he practices law and dreams about making good use of his BFA in oil painting.

David James' newest book, *Wiping Stars from Your Sleeves,* was published by Shanti Arts books in 2021. More than thirty of his one-act plays have been produced in the U.S. and Ireland. James teaches at Oakland Community College.

Jenny Kalahar is the editor and publisher of *Last Stanza Poetry Journal.* She is the founding leader of Last Stanza Poetry Association in  Elwood, Indiana, now in its tenth year. Jenny and her husband, poet Patrick, are used and rare booksellers. She was the humor columnist for *Tails Magazine* for several years and the treasurer for Poetry Society of Indiana. Author of fourteen books, she was twice nominated for a Pushcart Prize and once for Best of the Net. Her poems have been published in *Tipton Poetry Journal, Indiana Voice Journal, Trillium, Polk Street Review, Flying Island,* and in several anthologies and newspapers. Her works can be found on poemhunter.com and *INverse,* Indiana's poetry archive. Through Stackfreed Press, she has published books for numerous authors. Contact her at laststanza@outlook.com

Patrick Kalahar is a used and rare bookseller with his wife, Jenny, and a book conservationist. He is a veteran, world traveler, avid reader, and book collector. He is a member of Last Stanza Poetry Association. His poems have been published in *Tipton Poetry Journal, Flying Island, Rail Lines, The Moon and Humans, Polk Street Review, Northwest Indiana Literary Journal,* and *A Disconsolate Planet.* Patrick can be seen as an interviewee in the Emmy-winning documentary *James Whitcomb Riley: Hoosier Poet,* and he gives costumed and scholarly readings as Edgar Allan Poe.

JL Kato is a retired newspaper copy editor. He is the former poetry editor of *Flying Island* and a former president of Brick Street Poetry, an arts organization that plans literary events. He lives in Beech Grove, Indiana.

Jordan Krais is a poet from the north shore of Long Island. He's spent most of the last two years roaming the river near his home. You can find him on Instagram @captain_hawthorne where he posts pictures of the river and the stuff he types on his typewriter.

Norbert Krapf, former Indiana Poet Laureate, has two new books coming out this year, *Spirit Sister Dance*, poems about his stillborn sister  (Jan. 25, 1950) and the prose memoir *Homecomings*, which covers the fifty years of his writing and publishing life. The poem on the remedies of his maternal ancestor is based on journal passages in his 1996 book *Finding the Grain: Pioneer German Journals and Letters from Dubois County, Indiana*, which also includes the photo of the John L. Betz farmhouse.

Lucy J. Madison is a novelist, credited screenwriter, and poet from Connecticut. *I.V. Poems,* her debut collection of poetry, centers on time, place, and relationships. *Personal Foul* was named one of the Ten Best Lesbian Sports Romances by *The Lesbian Review. In the Direction of the Sun* was named a 2017 Best Book Awards Finalist, while her most recent novel, *A Recipe for Love*, received great reviews from *Curve*  *Magazine* and *Publisher's Weekly Booklife.* Her latest literary fiction novel, *Raising Artemis,* will be released in 2022. *Raising Artemis* is a poignant and uplifting story about the extraordinary soul connection between pets and people...as only a cat could tell it. She's a member of the National League of American Pen Women and resides in Connecticut and Provincetown, MA. lucyjmadison.com @lucyjmadison labradorpublishing.com

Guna Moran is an international poet and book reviewer. His poems are published in more than 150 international magazines, journals, webzines, blogs, newspapers, anthologies and have been translated into thirty languages around the world. He has three poetry books to his credit. He lives in Assam, India.

Jacob R. Moses (AKA Jack M. Freedman) is a poet and spoken word artist from Staten Island, NY. Publications featuring his work span the globe. Countries in which poems found homes include USA, Canada, UK, Ireland, France, The Netherlands, Ukraine, Nigeria, South Africa, Mauritius, Pakistan, India, Bangladesh, Singapore, and Thailand. He penned  the full-length poetry book, *Grimoire* (ii Publishing, 2021). Currently, he is pursuing a MA in English and Creative Writing at Southern New Hampshire University (SNHU).

Rich Murphy's *Meme Measure*, a collection of poems, will be published by Wipf and Srock in 2022. His poems included in *Last Stanza* are also in *Meme Measure*. His poetry has won The Poetry Prize at Press Americana twice: *Americana* (2013) and *The Left Behind* (2021), and Gival Press Poetry Prize for *Voyeur* (2008). *Space Craft* by Wipf and Stock came out 2021. Books *Prophet Voice Now*, essays by Common Ground Research Network, and *Practitioner Joy*, poetry by Wipf and Stock 2020. He has published seven other collections of poetry. He is a guest lecturer at Massachusetts College of Art and design.

Sheila E. Murphy is the recipient of the Gertrude Stein Award for her book *Letters to Unfinished J.* (Green Integer Press, 2003). Her most recent book is *Golden Milk* (Luna Bisonte Prods, 2020). *Reporting Live from You Know* Where won the Hay(na)Ku Poetry Book Prize Competition (Meritage Press (U.S.A.) and xPress(ed) (Finland), 2018). Also in 2018, Broken Sleep Books brought out the book *As If To Tempt the Diatonic Marvel from the Ivory.*

Lylanne Musselman is an award-winning poet, playwright, and visual artist. Her work has appeared in *Pank, The New Verse News, Tipton*

Poetry Journal, Flying Island, Rose Quartz Magazine, Last Stanza Poetry Journal, and *The Ekphrastic Review,* among others. Musselman's work has appeared in many anthologies, including *The Indianapolis Anthology* (Belt Publishing, 2021). She is the author of six chapbooks, including *Paparazzi for the Birds* (Red Mare 16, 2018) and is the co-author of *Company of Women: New and Selected Poems* (Chatter House Press, 2013). She is author of the full-length poetry collection, *It's Not Love, Unfortunately* (Chatter House Press, 2018). Musselman is a four-time Pushcart Prize nominee, and her poems are included in the INverse Poetry Archive, a collection of Hoosier poets, housed at the Indiana State Library. She teaches writing of all stripes at Ivy Tech Community College. Musselman is currently working on several poetry manuscripts.

James Nolan's latest book of poetry is *Nasty Water: Collected New Orleans Poems* (University of Louisiana at Lafayette Press, 2018). Previous collections are *Why I Live in the Forest, What Moves Is Not the Wind,* and *Drunk on Salt,* and his translations include volumes of Neruda and Gil de Biedma. His *Flight Risk* won the 2018 Next-Generation Indie Book Award for Best Memoir. The three books of his fiction have been

awarded a Faulkner-Wisdom Gold Medal, an Independent Publishers Book Award, and a Next-Generation Indie Book Award. The recipient of an NEA and two Fulbright fellowships, he has taught at universities in San Francisco, Florida, Barcelona, Madrid, Beijing, as well as in his native New Orleans. www.pw.org/directory/writers/james_nolan

Thomas Alan Orr's most recent collection is *Tongue to the Anvil: New and Selected Poems* (Restoration Press). He has recent work appearing in *The Sun, The Merton Seasonal,* and *Appalachian Witness* (Pine Mountain Sand & Gravel). He is a two-time nominee for the Pushcart Prize.

Jacky Pugh grew up in Liverpool and ended up in Cornwall, the far southwest. She worked as a nurse and teacher, and recently retired from full time work to find time to focus on poetry, arts, and crafts. She has always written poems and loves reading poetry and learning about it.

Marjorie Sadin has four books of poetry, including three chapbooks: *The Cliff Edge* by Modern Images and *Struck by Love* and *In a Closet* by Goldfish Press, also *Vision of Lucha,* a full-length book by Goldfish Press. She has been published in numerous magazines, including *The Jewish Women's Literary Annual, Snakeskin Press, Nailed Magazine, Subsync Press Poem of the Month, Bellowing Arc Press,* among many others. She lives and reads her poetry in the Washington, DC area.

Prartho Sereno has four prizewinning poetry collections including *Indian Rope Trick, Elephant Raga, Call from Paris,* and her illustrated collection, *Causing a Stir: The Secret Lives and Loves of Kitchen Utensils. She* served as fourth Poet Laureate of Marin County 2015-17, and taught poem-making to children as a Poet in the Schools for over 21 years, as well as to adults at the College of Marin. She currently teaches The Poetic Pilgrimage: Poem-Making as Spiritual Practice at www.prarthosereno.com

Mary Sexson is author of the award-winning book, *103 in the Light, Selected Poems 1996-2000 (*Restoration Press*),* and co-author of *Company of Women, New and Selected Poems* (Chatter House Press). Her poetry has appeared in *Tipton Poetry Journal, Laureate, Literary Journal of Arts for Lawrence, Flying Island Journal, New Verse News,* and *Last Stanza Poetry Journal,* among others. Sexson's poems are also included in various anthologies. Her most recent work is in *Reflections on Little Eagle Creek Anthology*, and *Anti-Heroin Chic* (October 2021). Her work is part of INverse Poetry Archives for Hoosier Poets.

Jeffrey Spahr-Summers is a poet, writer, photographer, and publisher. His work can be found at www.jeffreyspahrsummers.com

Michael E. Strosahl was born and raised in Moline, Illinois, just blocks from the Mississippi River. He has written poetry since youth. After moving to Tipton, Indiana, he participated in a poetry reading on a dare at the Barnes & Noble in Westfield, Indiana, 2001. He then became active in the Indiana poetry scene, becoming involved in what is now known as the Poetry Society of Indiana. He traveled the state in search of small groups that met in living rooms, libraries, and coffee houses, and he started groups in communities where he found  none. He served the PSI as Membership Chair and eventually as President. In 2018, he relocated to Jefferson City, MO, beginning his search anew for kindred spirits to inspire and draw energy from. He currently co-hosts a monthly critique group in the capital city and is a member of Last Stanza Poetry Association.

Diana Thoresen is a Russian-Australian writer who works on free energy research and development. She is a Managing Editor/Cover Artist for the world's first multilingual anthology in 22 languages, *Voracious Polyglots.*

Theresa Timmons is a storyteller, gardener, dog lover, and mischievous  "rider-of-roller-coasters" grandmother. When she is not playing with playdough or dancing in a tutu with the grandkids, she does a little writing. Theresa was a humor columnist for the *Anderson Herald* for ten years, and is a member of the Last Stanza Poetry Association. She was nominated for a 2022 Pushcart Prize in poetry.

Mary Kay Turner is an eternal student and her current fields of study are outrageousness, writing, and not taking herself too seriously. Next semester: fallibility, surrender, and genuine kindness. These are among her first published poems.

Rp Verlaine, a retired English teacher living in New York City, has an MFA in creative writing from City College. He has several collections of poetry including *Femme Fatales Movie Starlets & Rockers* (2018) and

Lies From The Autobiography 1-3 (2018-2020). His newest collection, *Imagined Indecencies,* will appear in early 2022. His poetry has appeared in *Atlas Poetica, The Linnet's Wings, Moving Images, Scissortail Quarterly, Chrysanthemum Literary Anthology, Last Stanza Poetry Journal, Booze Cocktails, Wales Haiku Journal, The Mainichi, Splintered Disorder Press, Rigorous, The South Shore Review, The Local Train, Proletaria, Haikuniverse, Scry of Lust 2* anthology, *Rudderless Mariner, Humankind Journal, The Wild Word, Under The Basho, Plum Tree Tavern, Fresh Out Magazine, Scissortail Quarterly, Prune Juice, Incense Dreams, Last Leaves, Blazevox, Buk 100, Pikers Press, Poems' bout Love & Hate* anthology, *Stardust Haiku, Heart of Flesh. Upwrite Mag., Cajun Mutt Press, Runcible Spoon, The South Shore Review, Lothlorien Press, Dumpster Fire Press, The Dope Fiend Daily, Mad Swirl, Fleas On The Dog, Yellow Mamma, Otoliths, Alien Buddha, Ygdrasil, Ink Pantry, Dirty Kids Press, Flights, Dreich, Pop The Culture Pill, Trouville Review, Better Than Starbucks, Failed Haiku, Autumn Moon Journal.*

J. T. Whitehead was Editor in Chief of *So It Goes: The Literary Journal of the Kurt Vonnegut Memorial Library.* He is a *Pushcart Prize*-nominated short story author, a seven-time *Pushcart Prize*-nominated poet, and was the winner of the *Margaret Randall Poetry Prize* (2015). Whitehead has published over 280 poems and prose works in over 100 literary journals and small press publications, including *The Lilliput Review, Outsider, Slipstream, Left Curve, The Broadkill Review, The Iconoclast, Gargoyle,* and *Poetry Hotel.* His first full-length collection of poetry, *The Table of the Elements*, was nominated for the *National Book Award* in 2015.

Matthew Whybrew is an Indiana-based writer and mental health clinician. He grew up on a farm in rural north-central Indiana where he spent much of his time in nature and its beauty. His experiences in the mental health field as well as his humble upbringing have colored his writing and other artistic endeavors. Matthew often draws from his own struggles with mental health to create relatable pieces that may be helpful to another. His mission is to bring meaningful and wholesome life to those with whom he interacts. This will be Matthew's first published poem.

Marilyn J Wolf is a poet, author, wanderer, and is always curious. *In Celebration of the Death of Faeries* is her first book; she is currently editing a second.

One of Bloomington's finest and most outspoken poets, **Hiromi**  **Yoshida** is a finalist for the 2019 New Women's Voices Poetry Prize, and a semifinalist for the 2020 Gerald Cable Book Award. She is a poetry reader for *Flying Island Journal* and for *Plath Profiles*, and the diversity consultant for the Writers Guild at Bloomington. She is also a freelance writer and editor, who has contributed to *Limestone Post*, *The Ryder*, and *The Bloomingtonian*. Her poems have secured Pushcart Prize and Best of the Net nominations and have been added to the INverse Poetry Archive. She is the author of three poetry chapbooks: *Icarus Redux*, *Epicanthus*, and *Icarus Burning*. As a child, she had learned to value women superheroes over damsels in distress.

Judy Young is a lifelong Elwood poet and member of Last Stanza Poetry Association, the Poetry Society of Indiana, and the National Federation of State Poetry Societies. She is married with five  children, nine grandbabies, and seven great-grandchildren. She is the author of *Wild Wood* and *Moonset,* and has been published in *Tipton Poetry Journal, Indiana Voice Journal,* and in several anthologies and journals. She is a nature advocate and tree enthusiast.